50 0296704 2

362

D0303480

Classical World series

SLAVERY IN
CLASSICAL GR

ST. MATTHIAS
LIBRARY

N.R.E. Fisher

st date

UWE, BRISTOL   B1087.6.93
Printing & Stationery Services

UWE BRISTOL
WITHDRAWN
LIBRARY SERVICES

First published in 1993 by
Bristol Classical Press
an imprint of
Gerald Duckworth & Co. Ltd
48 Hoxton Square
London N1 6PB

© 1993 by N.R.E. Fisher

All rights reserved. No part of this publication
may be reproduced, stored in a retrieval system, or
transmitted, in any form or by any means, electronic,
mechanical, photocopying, recording or otherwise,
without the prior permission of the publisher.

ISBN 1-85399-134-1

A catalogue record for this book
is available from the British Library

Printed and bound in Great Britain by
The Cromwell Press Ltd, Melksham, Wiltshire

Contents

List of Illustrations

Fig. 1 Tombstone of an Athenian boy. [Courtesy of Conze, Attische Grabrelief, Vienna]

Fig. 2 A *symposion* scene, on a sixth-century Attic black-figure Siana cup. [Courtesy of the Museum für Kunst und Gewerbe, Hamburg]

Fig. 3 Olive-pickers, on a late sixth-century Attic black-figure vase (*amphora*), by the Antimenes Painter. [Courtesy of the British Museum]

Fig. 4 A deep mine-shaft from Thorikos. [Courtesy of J. Ellis Jones]

Fig. 5 A photograph of one of the largest and best-planned surface workshops with ore-washeries, from the Laurion area. [Courtesy of J. Ellis Jones]

Fig. 6 A reconstruction drawing of the ore-washing process. [Courtesy of J. Ellis Jones]

Fig. 7 Shackles from the fourth-century BC, found in the Laurion area. [Courtesy of the Bergakademie, Freiberg]

Fig. 8 Manufacturing scene in a Foundry, on an early fifth-century Attic cup by the Foundry Painter. [Courtesy of Berlin Staatliche Museen]

Fig. 9 Slave girl and mistress, on a mid-fifth-century Attic white-ground oil vessel (*lekythos*), probably by the Nikon Painter. [Courtesy of the Musées royaux d'art et d'histoire, Brussels]

Fig. 10 A scene from a gymnasium, on an Attic mixing-bowl (*kalyx-krater*), c. 500 BC by the painter Euphronios. [Courtesy of the Berlin Staatliche Museen]

Fig. 11 Tattooed slave-women, on an Attic water-vessel (*hydria*) by by the Aegisthus Painter, c. 470 BC [Courtesy of the Louvre Museum, Paris]

Fig. 12 A *symposion*-scene on an Attic cup by the Foundry Painter. [Courtesy of Corpus Christi College, Cambridge]

Preface

Scope

The purpose of this small book on a very large subject is to introduce readers to the major issues raised by the institution of slavery in classical Greece. It focuses on slavery and other types of non-free labour in the period of independent city-states, from their formation around the time of Homer to their loss of political independence in the later fourth century BC; there is no attempt to consider here slavery in Mycenaean Greece or in Greece in the time of the Hellenistic kingdoms. Further, the nature of the evidence forces us to concentrate above all on slavery and serfdom in two, or perhaps three, cities: helots in Sparta and chattel slaves in Athens, with some intriguing glimpses of slaves on the island of Chios.

Study of slavery in any society where it was of considerable economic importance involves asking two separable – but connected – types of questions: first, how the institution of slavery actually worked, and how it was experienced by slaves and by slaveowners; and second, what were its effects on all other aspects of the society, above all on the dominant sets of ideas ('ideologies') of the members of the society. For classical Greece, unfortunately, we are almost totally denuded of evidence giving us access to the slaves' point of view, and most of our evidence indeed comes from the literate élites of the city-states. Furthermore slavery was, I believe, one of the most important and determining elements in Greek society. For these reasons therefore this book considers the effects of slavery on the ideas and social values of the slave-owning free population as much as it does the operations of the institution itself.

I have quoted ancient evidence throughout (in my own translations), and given a number of references to other passages. To facilitate further study of the evidence, I have referred, in the form *GARS*, to passages which are included in Thomas Wiedemann's useful source book *Greek and Roman Slavery*.

Acknowledgements

I am extremely grateful to the Series Editor Michael Gunningham, for inviting me to write the book, and for taking infinite pains to improve its structure and expression; to Anton Powell, Tracey Rihll and, at a later stage, Thomas Wiedemann, for reading drafts and making very many helpful suggestions on matters of substance, presentation and bibliography; and to my wife Sarah and my daughter Kate for helping to sharpen the presentation and clarify the arguments. None is to be supposed to agree with my arguments, let alone share responsibility for my errors.

N.R.E.F.
University of Wales, Cardiff
1993

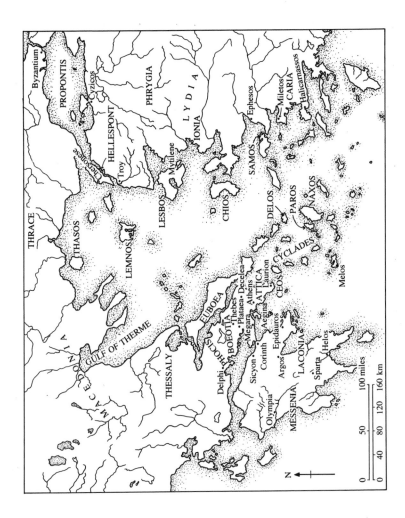

Classical
Greece

THRACE

MACEDONIA

Byzantium

PROPONTIS

Chalcedon

Cyzicos

HELLESPONT

PHRYGIA

Troy

L Y D I A

IONIA

Mytilene

LESBOS

Ephesos

Miletos

CARIA

Halicarnassos

SAMOS

CHIOS

THASOS

LEMNOS

DELOS

PAROS

NAXOS

CYCLADES

CEOS

GULF OF THERME

EUBOEA

THESSALY

PHOCIS

BOEOTIA

Delphi

Thebes

Plataea

Decelea

Megara

Athens

ATTICA

Aegina

Laurion

Sicyon

Corinth

Epidauros

Argos

Olympia

MESSENIA

LACONIA

Helos

Sparta

Melos

N

0   50   100 miles
0   40   80   120   160 km

Chapter 1

Definitions and Problems: Chattel Slaves, Serfs, and the Concept of a Slave-Society

Scholars of classical Greece and visitors to Greece have always admired – and with good reason – that civilization's major achievements: the splendid buildings and works of art, the profound works of literature and philosophy, and the development of new political ideas and institutions, above all, the ideas of freedom, active citizenship, and participatory democracy. One could hardly overstate the influence of such Greek achievements on the subsequent history of the West. But it would be wrong to ignore or underestimate their darker side. We must ask how the material wealth and leisure the Greeks enjoyed were created, and what exploitations of other human beings enabled the male citizens of the Greek *polis* (plural *poleis*, 'city-state') to participate in government and other cultural activities. To put it bluntly, can we say that any of these institutions, ideas and works of art (e.g., democracy, Sophocles' plays, Aristotle's philosophy, the Parthenon) would have taken the form they did had the Greeks not employed widespread slave-labour? This book will suggest that the answer is probably 'no', and in two distinct senses. First, unfree labour, of one type or another, contributed to the production of much of the wealth and the artistic objects; at the same time it helped wealthy and educated men to devote their leisure to politics, creativity or the pursuit of physical pleasures. Second, the consciousness of the division between slaves and free men was one of Greek society's most fundamental and determining ideas, one which affected profoundly many of the habits of thought and 'ideologies' of Greeks of all social classes on a wide range of different topics.

To explore these issues involves asking a number of further questions. We must first define key terms. What do we understand by the terms 'slaves' and 'slavery', and how do we distinguish 'chattel slaves' from 'serfs' or 'debt-bondsmen'? Then we have to raise factual questions about Greek societies. Roughly how many slaves or serfs were there in these societies? What work did they do? How were they treated? After that we may be able to approach the larger questions: were all ancient Greek societies equally 'dependent' on unfree-labour? How did

1

slavery affect the Greeks' views of human nature, of the difference between men and women, between Greeks and non-Greeks, and of the proper shape a society should have? Critical as these questions are, they are difficult to answer, and they continue to produce controversy and disagreement among historians.

There are at least two important reasons for this continuing debate. One reason is the inadequacy – often the extreme inadequacy – of the sources available for the study. Reliable statistics on the total numbers of slaves in any *polis* do not exist, and there is very limited – and often very problematic – evidence for such matters as slave-prices, the proportion of unfree and free people in various occupations, or the numbers of slaves 'manumitted', that is, given their freedom by their master. There are major debates on central questions, for example, the role of slave-labour in agriculture. Sophisticated statistical work on the profitability of slavery is ruled out (though one may note that where more abundant evidence might seem to exist, especially in the southern states of the USA, such work does not readily produce agreement). Furthermore, such discussions and incidental references as we do have on relations between masters and slaves, and on the effects of slavery on their ideas and ideologies, are almost entirely produced by and for the male masters, not the slaves. It is very difficult to trace the thoughts and feelings of the slaves themselves.

A second reason for controversy arises more from the continuing contemporary relevance of debates about slavery and other forms of labour, and from the different approaches and political views of different 'schools' of historians. Some, especially those related to the Marxist tradition, tend to concentrate rather on the economic structures of a society, in particular on the 'class-war' and the definition of classes in relation to the means of production. 'Marxists' may hold that these class-relations are the determining factors in the explanation of a society's basic structure and its major developments rather than issues of status or dominant ideas. Similarly, such historians show special sympathy for the downtrodden underclasses in history, and emphasise the cruelty and pervasiveness of 'exploitation', while playing down any possibilities of good or humane relations between masters and slaves, or between large landowners and peasants or serfs. Other historians, perhaps deriving their approach more from the sociologist Max Weber, prefer to place as much weight on the idea of status as on class: such historians may emphasise the degrading nature of master–slave relations as much or more than their economic exploitation. More conservative or idealistic historians may place weight on the ways in which some slaves were integrated (partially, at least) into the family life of their masters, or were encouraged through the hope and practice of manumission to develop more human relations with their masters, and to win some form of freedom. All these approaches, it seems to me, have some validity, and it must remain in part a matter of one's individual historical or political principles and priorities where one chooses to place most emphasis. Historians, while they must strive for maximum objectivity and accuracy, cannot escape from 'ideological' bias. Nor should they avoid awareness of the continuing significance of these debates; for example, proper emphasis on the evils of slavery, whether in the ancient world or in the Americas, should not be allowed to mask other forms of hardship or exploitation, such as conditions among the landless poor in non-industrial societies or the industrial working classes; nor should it allow other forms of ideological oppression to be forgotten, such as racialism, in the twentieth as in previous centuries.

Definitions

Definitions of a slave-society, and of the various types of non-free labour such as chattel slavery, serfdom, and debt-bondage, are matters of argument, and the argument reflects the different approaches mentioned above. Classical Greece saw the development of two broadly different types of societies: those where non-free labour was predominantly chattel slavery, and those where some form of state serfdom predominated. Sparta is the best known example of the second, Athens of the first.

A slave-society is usually held to be more than a community where numbers of slaves exist; there must be a substantial contribution by slaves to the wealth-production of that society. Slaves have existed in innumerable societies in human history, but relatively few of these societies can be safely classified as slave-societies. One definition of a slave-society is one in which slaves played an important part in production, and formed at least a substantial proportion of the total population, for example about 20% (e.g. Hopkins, *Conquerors and Slaves* 99). Alternatively, one may concentrate on the idea of productive work and say that a slave-society is one where the main labour providing the surplus production for the ruling class or the élite is slave-labour (so Finley, *Ancient Slavery and Modern Ideology* 77ff., and de Ste. Croix, *Class Struggle* 52ff.). In large-scale societies for which there are good statistics, particularly the New World societies with large-scale African slavery, slaves formed about 25-33% of the total population, performing most of the agricultural and other work from which the rich – above all the planters – derived their wealth. In a 'slave-society', it is not necessary for the majority of the free men to own slaves, and in the southern states of America, for example, most of the free population were poor white farmers with no slaves. In the case of Athens, as we shall see in chapter 4, there are debates on two crucial questions: how far slave-labour was used in agriculture, and how far slave-owning extended to the poorer peasants and manufacturers. While we cannot recover accurate population figures, it does seem highly probable that of all the civilizations of the ancient world, it is only classical Athens, probably a number of other Greek *poleis*, and Roman Italy, which can safely be considered 'slave-societies' to be compared with Brazil, the Caribbean and the USA.

Useful and widely accepted definitions of serfdom, debt-bondage and chattel slavery have been offered by the League of Nations Slavery Convention of 1926 and the Supplementary Convention of the United Nations of 1956 (they are quoted and discussed by de Ste. Croix, *Class Struggle* 134ff.). **Serfdom** is defined (in the 1956 Convention) as *the tenure of land whereby the tenant is by law, custom or agreement bound to live and labour on land belonging to another person and render some determinate services to such other person, whether for reward or not, and is not free to change his status.* Some historians confine the term serf to the feudal societies of the Middle Ages; but it seems reasonable to use the term to apply to the broader category of tenants suggested by this definition, which has existed in many societies. The essence of the definition is that serfs are relatively unfree peasants who are tied, often hereditarily, and by law or agreement, to work land which they do not themselves own. Although responsible for maintaining themselves from this land, they have other fixed dues or services to pay to their lord or master. One further addition to the definition is needed if it is to be applied to the 'state' or 'community' serfs found in Greek states such as Sparta. This would state that some 'serfs', like the Spartan helots, may be owned by the state, while the lands to which they are tied are owned by individual landowners. In many cases the origin of such serf-status lies in the conquest of a territory by invaders who imposed it on the defeated inhabitants.

Debt-bondage is defined by the 1956 Convention as *the status or condition resulting from a pledge by a debtor of his personal services or those of a third person under his control as a security for a debt, where the value reasonably assessed of those services is not applied to the liquidation of the debt or the length and nature of these services are not respectively limited and defined.* This definition perhaps does not sufficiently distinguish between debt-bondage, and slavery for debts. A debt-bondsman may be a debtor who pledges to provide crops or labour for his creditor, with the hope (however distant or unlikely) of being one day able to pay off the debt and become free again. Enslavement for debts, on the other hand, means that the debtor becomes permanently the slave of his creditor.

Two definitions of **chattel slavery** need discussion. One focuses on the nature of the power exercised by the individual master on the slave, the other on the effects of this power on the slave. The first is that of the League of Nations' 1926 Convention: *the status or condition of a person over whom any or all of the powers attaching to the right of ownership are exercised* – the phrasing was designed to include all those who are effectively seen as the personal property of their masters. This is in fact quite close to Aristotle's discussion in his *Politics* (1.2 = *GARS* 2) of a slave as someone who belongs to his master completely, as an 'animate piece of property' as well as a human being, and can be seen as a tool. One obvious mark of being the property of another is that one may be bought and sold. This definition in terms of personal ownership helpfully clarifies the essential differences between chattel slaves and state-serfs like the Spartan helots, who typically worked on an individual's estate, but were partly the property of the state and could not be sold without its permission. In two ways, state-serfs, like other serfs, were better off than chattel slaves: they were less likely to have lost all family connections, to be prevented from forming new relationships, or to have them disrupted by individual sales; and they were expected to perform specific work on the estate to which they were tied, and were to a lesser extent at the mercy or whim of their master. On the other hand, the chances of being freed may well have been higher when the choice was that of the individual master, not of the community.

This definition, however, does not bring out other essential aspects that are common to most types of chattel slavery. The other definition to be quoted is that argued for by Patterson in his *Slavery and Social Death: slavery is the permanent, violent, domination of natally alienated and generally dishonoured persons*. Here *permanent* means that the condition is likely to last till death and that there is no agreed condition that the slave could satisfy so as to claim a right to be freed – though of course his master may in fact choose to set him free. *Violent* refers to the element of force – actual or latent – inherent in the relationship. The Greeks, like other slaveowners, saw that one crucial difference between slave and free was that slaves were answerable with their bodies for their offences, and were in fact regularly whipped and could legally be tortured.

Domination picks up the point emphasised in the League of Nations' definition that slaves have to do everything they are told. *Natally alienated* indicates that slaves have no 'birth-rights', and do not 'belong' in the society in which they are enslaved (whether they came to it as captives, bought property, or were bred there); rather they remain permanently foreign, 'outsiders', having no social identity. Those who are enslaved during adult life often have their previous identity formally removed in the process of sale: they are stripped of their clothes, their former names, their kin, their nationality, and even their personality. Patterson calls this process 'social death', after which a new life begins with a different name and identity and very few, if any, rights. Such an experience was bound to be traumatic, and to a degree that is hard to imagine. Finally, Patterson's definition places at the centre of the experience of being a slave an almost complete state of *dishonour*, which is constantly and deliberately reinforced by his or her master.

These definitions emphasise – rightly, I believe – the completeness of the power exercised by slaveowners, and the dishonour and disorientation inflicted on the slaves. As we shall see later, there is much evidence in our Greek sources which suggests that slaveowners held contradictory attitudes, that crude assertions of power and brutality co-existed with more humane and warm relationships and the granting of some limited honour and the hope of freedom, at least to a minority of the slaves. How far such suggestions of limited humanity can mitigate the essential brutality, contempt and exploitation inherent in the institution remains a matter of debate.

Greek terms for slaves

Despite the apparent simplicity of a broad distinction between chattel slaves and state-serfs, the actual terms used by the Greeks for their dependent labour are bafflingly complex, and also remarkably haphazard. There are a great many terms used only to refer to specific groups of 'serfs' in particular places, as will be mentioned in chapter 3. Of the terms in more general use, many are applied equally to chattel slaves and helots, and some terms may be used of those of even more varied legal status. The terms which from the fifth century on most commonly indicate slave status as opposed to free are *douleia* (slavery), and *doulos* (slave) as opposed to *eleutheria, eleutheros* (freedom, free man). *Douloi* are usually full-scale chattel slaves. Yet authors often refer to the helots or to other 'state-serfs' casually as *douloi*, and the term is frequently used – by rhetorical extension – of political 'slavery', of subjects to a tyrant, or of 'allied' cities dominated by an imperial power like fifth-century Athens. One term used only of human beings seen as property is the curious word *andrapodon*: formed on the model of *tetrapodon*, 'four-footed creature'; it means literally 'man-footed creature' and is only used in the neuter, referring to a human being as an animal or a thing, to be bought and sold. Other commonly-used terms refer to the function of the non-free person. From the Greek work *oikos* (household) comes the term *oiketes* (compare 'houseboy'); or a slave may be called a *therapon* (servant), an *akolouthos* (attendant or follower) or simply a *soma* (body). Another term that may be used of a slave, with a demeaning implication, is *anthropos* (human being), suggesting that he or she is merely a human being with no further identity. A term with an even more obviously humiliating function, and one which is found in many slave-systems, is *pais* (child, boy or girl); applied to slaves of any age, it reminds them that they can never be treated as free or independent adults. Two passages from Athenian comedy bring out well the implications of this usage. A fragment of fourth-century comedy shows a fictional house-slave expressing his bitterness and resentment at being called 'Boy', especially by some drunken adolescent at a party, when the slave has to bring on the potties, and to look at the half-eaten food, while risking chastisement as a 'glutton' if he tries to eat any of the left-overs (Athenaeus, 262d = *GARS* 80, p. 80). Another comic passage, from a play of Aristophanes (*Wasps* 1296-8), humorously justifies calling an old slave *pais*, since, like children, slaves of all ages were likely to be beaten, with a pun suggesting an etymological connection between *pais* and *paiein* (to beat). This last point also reminds us that regular beating of children (and probably of wives too) was a much more standard and generally accepted feature of family life in the ancient world (and elsewhere) than in the contemporary western family.

Sources

Slaves were everywhere to be seen in Greek society, and references to them, and the use of the slave-free polarity, run throughout all our source-material. Most of the literary sources presuppose slavery, refer casually to slaves, or use the slave-free distinction as argument or illustration. Often they may presuppose stereotypes and conventions, rather than social realities. At all times such sources need to be interpreted both in relation to the conventions of their literary genre and to the expectations of their audiences. Extended defences of slavery and discussions of its problems, however, are relatively rare. Treatises on 'household management' included advice on how to select, train and manage slaves, and we have two short treatments, one by Xenophon, written perhaps around 360 BC, and one stemming from the Aristotelian school. In Book 1 of the *Politics* Aristotle himself offers a full-scale theoretical justification of slavery and a discussion of the differences between 'rule' over women, children and slaves (discussed in ch. 7). There are briefer discussions of some of these issues in various works by Plato, especially his *Laws*. The longest collection of scholarly discussions of slavery, from a great variety of lost works, comes in an extended section from Athenaeus' *Deipnosophistai* ('Intellectuals at Dinner'), a very long book written by an educated Greek living in Egypt under the Roman Empire c. AD 200 (262ff. = *GARS* 80). The work, in the form of learned conversations at an elaborate banquet, is a remarkably discursive discussion of all topics to do with dinner-parties and

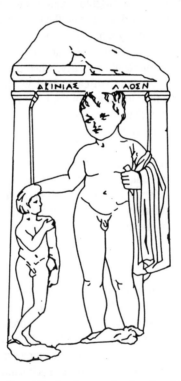

Fig. 1 Tombstone of an Athenian boy, resting hand on his (actually much older) slave *paidagogus*' head. In such cases slave status is indicated by the totally unrealistic size.

drinking-parties (the Greek *symposia*). Its chief value to us is that it contains innumerable, often lengthy, quotations from earlier poets, philosophers, dramatists, historians and so on.

Archaeological evidence has its contribution to make in this area, though it can tell us less about economic and social relationships involving slaves than about many other aspects of Greek history. Slaves seem to be depicted quite often on vases and sculptural monuments, although there are frequently problems in securely identifying the status of apparently 'low-class' figures. Excavations, field surveys, and comparative studies of the countryside can reveal much of the conditions and environment in which slaves and free alike worked and lived. Study of burials and burial goods may suggest changes in social structures and discrimination between different social classes, though suggestions of this sort are controversial and uncertain. Documents and other writings, mostly written on stone or other hard materials and found in excavations ('inscriptions'), are an invaluable source of information, especially on matters such as slave-prices, slave-occupations and manumissions. But the randomness and incompleteness of such records make their statistical use particularly hazardous.

Chapter 2

The Development of Chattel Slavery:
From Homer to Solon

Homer and the Dark Ages

The Homeric poems, which were perhaps completed in the last third of
the eighth century BC, present a number of fictional societies, above all
those of Troy, the Greek camp at Troy, and on Odysseus' island of Ithaca.
The poems purport to be set in the Greek heroic past, that is in what we
call the period of the Mycenaean Kingdoms of the Greek Bronze Age
(c. thirteenth-twelfth centuries BC). Whether or not there is any historical
reality underlying the main events portrayed in the poems, that is the
Trojan war and its aftermath, remains uncertain. But it seems clear that
the social and economic activities and institutions described or assumed
in the poems reflect the developing circumstances of the Greek communities of the 'Dark Ages', that is to say, of the ninth and more
especially the eighth centuries BC, much more than they do those of the
earlier Bronze Age. We learn from the archaeological evidence, and
above all from the 'Linear B Tablets' (documentary records written in
Greek found in the excavations from Mycenaean Palaces such as those
at Knossos, Mycenae and Pylos), that there were 'slaves' (*doero* = later
Greek *doulos*) in the Bronze Age kingdoms; but the economic conditions
and types of relationships appear quite different from those in the
Homeric poems. The eighth-century world was overwhelmingly agricultural but, as we can now see from archaeological evidence, it had
substantial contacts with the wider Mediterranean, which took the varied
forms of trade, piracy, alliances and guest-friendships.

In Homer's societies, in Troy and Ithaca, we find what appear to
be slaves, though it is difficult to classify them accurately or be sure how
many different types were involved. They are usually called *dmoes*
(masculine), *dmoiai* (feminine), though the later standard terms for slave
and slavery, *doulos and douleia* do occur occasionally. Nearly all of
them are seen working for the households of the 'Kings', that is the
nobles or 'Big Men', mostly as male herdsmen or as female domestics.
In arable agriculture large landowners, and even some poor farmers,

10

seem to make some use of hired 'day-labourers' (*thes*, plural *thetes*), who are not slaves. For example, the evil suitor Eurymachos insulted Odysseus (disguised as a beggar) by asking him whether he would work for him as a *thes*, on a far-distant field picking up stones for a wall, and then suggesting he was too lazy for hard work (*Odyssey* 18.356-64). Often, however, the status of 'workers' in agricultural scenes is simply not made clear, as for example in the scenes depicted on the shield of Achilles in Book 18 of the *Iliad*. In general, the Homeric poems largely ignore the agricultural conditions and ordinary lives of poorer 'peasants' who may or may not have had specific ties or obligations towards the nobles; such peasants form presumably the vast majority of the troops who fight and die in the battles which fill the *Iliad*.

Real life peasants were, it seems, the target audience of Hesiod's poem *Works and Days*, which was composed c. 700 BC in the context of a small rural community in southern Boeotia. Hesiod's instructions, which are probably to be imagined as directed at the better-off peasants, often assume that these peasants will have one or more slaves (*dmoes*) available to perform various tasks throughout the year (e.g., 441-72 – ploughing, 597-600 – threshing). Reference is occasionally made as well to the use of short-term hired labour; after the grain is safely stored away, the peasant is advised to send away the *thes* (602-3). But Hesiod offers no clue as to the origins of his slaves.

The picture of slavery in Homer's poems suggests both similarities and differences when compared to those of the later classical period (fifth-fourth centuries BC). Some of the slaves of whose origins we hear were war-booty, to be owned by the victors, or sold, or given as gifts; others were captured by pirates or traders and sold. On such grounds, then, they seem to have been typically outsiders in the small communities where they are slaves, and hence might be thought essentially to be 'chattel slaves', the property of their masters, and 'natally alienated'. It is important to note, however, that they were as likely to be Greek as non-Greek. This is probably a major difference between the 'Homeric' and the classical period, where most slaves seem to have been non-Greek. Thus in the fullest Homeric account of a slave's origins, the swineherd Eumaios tells Odysseus how he was originally the son of a Greek 'King' on the island of Syros, but had been taken away as a boy almost by chance when his nurse, a Phoenician slavewoman, who had herself been captured by 'Taphian' pirates, eloped with Phoenician traders, taking the boy with her to fetch a good price elsewhere. The girl died on the voyage, but the Phoenician traders sold the boy to Odysseus' father on Ithaca (*Odyssey* 15.403-84). Whether, however, in this fictional society, let alone in the real eighth-century Greek communities, all slaves were 'outsiders', or whether it was possible or common for 'insiders' to become fully enslaved to their richer neighbours, is quite uncertain. Equally, the tendency in the *Odyssey* to present traders as non-Greeks (Phoenicians) or as in this case as marginal Greeks (Taphians) probably reflects nostalgic aristocratic prejudice rather than eighth-century realities.

Many of the slaves of the *Odyssey* seem to enjoy a firm, almost respectable, place in the household. Some have been granted limited property-rights, and the chance to marry and have a family life. They could enjoy long-standing relations of trust and loyalty with their masters. Eumaios is again an excellent example (cf. *Odyssey* Books 14 and 15). Hence it can be plausible to suppose that a destitute free man, a *thes*, only occasionally getting some hired labour, and otherwise begging, may be the most miserable being imaginable. This is perhaps implied by the dead Achilles' statement to Odysseus in the Underworld:

> Do not smooth over death to me, noble Odysseus.
> I would prefer to be on the land working as a *thes* for another,
> for a man without inheritance, who had a small livelihood,
> than to be a lord over all the dead who have perished.
>
> (*Odyssey* 11.489-91)

To be an accepted slave inside a prosperous household might seem preferable to being a landless hired labourer, insecurely attached to a poor household. But it may be that Achilles could not even imagine his ever being a slave, and a *thes* was the lowest being he could conceive of.

Thus in the *Odyssey* there is considerable scope for the domestic or herdsmen slaves to show independence, loyalty and friendships with their masters – or to break trust through idleness or disloyalty. The poem's central story of Odysseus' recovery of his household presents the triumph of the good over the bad, and the proper punishment of those who have been dishonouring the house. The identification of the loyal and the disloyal slaves, each receiving their respective deserts, plays an important part in the unfolding of the story. In our response to the close and emotionally charged relations between good and fairly successful slaves like Eumaios and good masters like Odysseus and his family, we should remember the needs of the plot, and the probability of idealisation of the hero, and of stereotyping of good and bad slaves. There are also many harsh elements in the picture. Masters expect to be obeyed unquestioningly; as Eumaios says, fearing a punishment even from a good master like Telemachos: 'the reproofs of masters are hard to bear' (*Odyssey* 17.187-8). The punishments meted out to the disloyal are deliberately savage and humiliating. Twelve (out of 50) slave-girls who had dishonoured the house by sleeping with the suitors are given the 'unclean' and 'most pitiable' death of a mass hanging (*Odyssey* 20.417-73). Melanthios the insolent goatherd who had happily served the suitors has his nose, ears, hands and feet cut off and his genitals fed to the dogs (*Odyssey* 22.474-7).

'Homeric' slaves may be Greek or foreign and may come from any class; it is perhaps not surprising then that there is no sign in the poems of an attempt to justify slavery as an institution in terms of the racial or social inferiority of slaves. A very revealing remark on the effect of being made a slave comes in Eumaios' comment on why the disloyal and lazy female slaves of the household have neglected to care for the old dog Argos, who lies on the dunghill and recognises, in his dying moments, the returning Odysseus:

> Domestic slaves (*dmoes*), when their lords no longer give them
>   commands,
> are then no longer willing to perform their proper tasks.
> For far-voiced Zeus removes half the goodness (*arete*)
> of a man, when the day of slavery (*doulion emar*) takes hold of
>   him.
>
> (*Odyssey* 17.320-3)

First, the phrase 'the day of slavery' (which occurs elsewhere in the poems) suggests an understanding of the traumatic shock of the initial enslavement (cf. above, p. 6). This is explored more sensitively in a number of passages in the *Iliad*, especially those where the enslavement of Andromache and other Trojan women is anticipated (e.g., *Iliad* 6.447-65, 24.725-34). On that day a person's former status and sense of worth are removed at a stroke. Second, the lines reflect the belief that slaves have – as a result, presumably, of this loss of status and identity – a diminished moral capacity; they have lost 'half' their capacity for good behaviour (*arete*) and for the honour that would come to them as a result. Hence slaves become, almost automatically, moral inferiors by the dishonouring experience of enslavement; they cannot be relied on to choose uncommanded to work for their households, or to show courage and seek honour for themselves. Consequently they need constant supervision, incentives and punishment. Their assumed failure to adopt voluntarily the ideals of their society, after their enslavement, thus helps to justify the measures of control adopted by their masters.

Third, this assessment of slaves' propensity to immorality and dishonour has to be modified by its very context. The fact that it is Eumaios, the brave slave who has chosen in great adversity to stay loyal to Odysseus and Telemachos, who makes this statement itself limits its applicability – it seems to be much less true of Eumaios or of other loyal slaves, though even they can never recover the full degrees of 'goodness' open to the free. This ambivalent picture suggests two things about the Homeric 'ideology' of slavery: it allows for the possibility for slaves to attain, through good behaviour, rewards and friendly relations with their masters, and it justifies the punishment of the disloyal. Slaves, though now (thanks to enslavement) prone to behave badly, do retain some capacity for moral choice.

The rise of the polis

Homer may perhaps have been creating his imaginary societies, out of predominantly eighth-century elements, at a time (c. 750-700 BC) when the Greek world was beginning to undergo a set of radical and varied changes, as we see above all from the archaeological record. Population was rising – though how rapidly is very much disputed. More land on the Greek mainland was being taken into cultivation, and perhaps increasingly used for arable rather than pastoral farming, and new crops were being introduced. *Poleis* were formed, as their boundaries were fixed, and single settlements identified as their centres, which were often fortified. Each individual *polis* identity was established by localised cult-sites, temples and associated myths. Writing was re-introduced into Greece, which helped later to produce a demand for the city's laws and regulations to be written on stone and displayed in public. Then over-population and the awareness, through trading contacts, of opportunities for land-acquisition overseas produced the lengthy process we call 'colonization' – the establishment of new Greek *poleis* all round the Mediterranean and the Black Sea. Partly in consequence of these developments and also, perhaps, as a result of changes in military equipment and deployment (hoplite armour and the hoplite phalanx), significant political developments occurred in a number of cities. In some, tyrannies were established; in others, new laws and constitutional bodies and procedures were adopted that gave a more systematic and regular participation in government to more of the 'people' – the non-aristocratic free male members of the community.

The part played by non-free labour in this complex set of economic and political developments remains obscure. It seems probable, however, that (leaving Sparta aside for the moment) causal links may be found between a steady growth of chattel slavery, a sharper distinction between slaves and free men, and initial moves towards wider popular participation in government and law. The evidence available largely concerns developments in sixth-century Athens, though there are hints of comparable developments elsewhere.

Athens at the time of Solon
Athens down to about 620 BC presents a rather odd picture, on the basis of the archaeological evidence and the sparse literary records. Athens did not establish any colonies, and there is no hint of serious political conflict before the attempted tyranny of Cylon and the laws of Draco (c. 630-620). There is an unresolved debate whether to interpret the archaeological record of burial customs and of pottery in the early seventh century in terms of an inward-looking, conservative, divided society, or of an innovative, insecure but fast-developing society. It seems likely that settlement patterns were changing fast as the interior of Attica was increasingly developed, and that this produced major disputes between rich and poor cultivators. Draco's laws seem to have exacerbated the agrarian crisis; by the time Solon was appointed to propose new laws (594 is the traditional date, though it may have been a few years later), the danger of civil wars and a tyranny was evidently great. One important result of Solon's laws seems to have been a clearer distinction between citizens, slaves and foreigners; and in more than one way his laws helped the creation of the Athenian model of a slave-society.

The economic crisis involved the relations between rich land-owners and peasants and the state, which itself was largely or wholly dominated by the richest aristocrats. More than one type of dependency of the poor on the rich was probably involved. Some peasants may have become heavily burdened with 'debts', that is, in what was still a pre-coinage economy, fixed obligations to provide crops and services to richer landowners; and in some cases failure to pay enough could involve actual slavery for these 'debts', whether in Attica or abroad. In that sense, there were both debt-bondsmen, and for some of these, ensuing slavery for debts. There was also a specific category called the *hektemoroi* or 'sixth-parters', peasants farming under permanent and perhaps inheritable conditions of 'sharecropping'. It is unclear whether, as Aristotle thought, the land such men tilled was regarded as owned by the rich, or by the peasants themselves (with a permanent obligation owed to the rich), or whether it may have been 'public land'. It is even unclear whether the sharecroppers paid one-sixth or five-sixths of the crop under these 'dues'. In any case, the concept of 'ownership' was not well defined, and it is likely that there were a number of different types and terms of dependence: for example, the *hektemoroi* may have worked what was considered 'public' land, and others (e.g., the 'clients' or *pelatai* also mentioned in Aristotle's account) may have share-cropped for private landowners. It is also likely that some or all of these dependent statuses were connected with the process, as population increased, of opening up more of the land in Attica to agriculture.

Hence it was not necessarily the case that all the *hektemoroi* in Solon's day had difficulties in paying these dues, or were very poor. Aristotle may have been right when he claimed that 'what was most difficult and bitter for the majority of people about the political system was the enslavement' (*Constitution of Athens* 2 = *GARS* 16), though in two different senses: for many it was the slave-like status of being a share-cropper that was intolerable; for others it was the serious threat, or even the reality, of being actually made a slave. In a world where newly-bought, foreign, slaves were more in evidence, those who felt they had a long-standing right to be members of the community of Athens demanded a sharper distinction be made between themselves and these newcomers, and resented being humiliated and treated as slaves by the rich either at work in the fields or more generally in social life.

Solon's laws, as far as we are able to reconstruct them, clearly addressed these problems. Several features of the laws may be mentioned. First, in what was known as the 'shaking off of burdens' (the *seisachtheia*), the peasant-citizen was more firmly established. No Athenian was henceforth to be enslaved in Athens and, in general, both debt-bondage and slavery for debts were abolished (no one could enter a debt-obligation giving his own person as security). Abolished too was the whole status of *hektemoros* (probably the land they had worked became the peasants' own in most, perhaps in all, cases). Solon himself summed up the freeing of the peasants in one of his poems, written after the passing of his laws:

> The earth, before enslaved, is now free.
> And I brought back to Athens to their god-given country
> many who had been sold, some unjustly,
> others justly, others fleeing from heavy
> necessity, no longer speaking the Attic tongue,
> as they had been wandering in many places.

> And those here, in this land, enduring shameful
> slavery, trembling at the ways of their masters,
> I set free.

> (Solon, fr. 36.10-15)

Second, Solon produced complex laws of adoption and inheritance, aimed as far as possible at preserving (given the basic Greek practice of equal division of estates between sons) a settled number of households. Third, citizens were encouraged to participate more actively in legal processes. They could now act as prosecutors, especially where offences were committed against the weaker members of society, or against citizens' fundamental status, or against the community as a whole; and they could act as jurors in the new Appeal Court. In particular, the famous Athenian law against *hybris* (text in Demosthenes, *Against Meidias* 21.47 = *GARS* 183), almost certainly a law of Solon's, sought to protect the ordinary citizen against *hybris*, that is, gratuitous or contemptuous behaviour, often involving violence and designed to humiliate or shame the victim. Such an offence was often committed by the rich during or after their drinking parties (*symposia*). At this period poor free men may have been vulnerable to such abuse. It has been plausibly suggested on the basis of illustrations on pots that in the archaic period low-status free men, such as the share-cropping 'clients' of the rich, performed – as 'uninvited guests' driven by their poverty – vulgar dances at *symposia*. Later such entertainers, who would clearly be vulnerable to drunken abuse, would largely be slaves or foreigners.

Solon's laws, then, sought to establish the peasant-citizens securely on their farms, to create stable and lasting households, to give them a slightly greater participation in government and the legal process, and to protect them by writing 'ordinances for good and bad man alike/providing straight justice for each man' (Solon, fr. 36.21-3). He thus sought to ensure that free-born Athenians were no longer humiliated or treated as 'slaves' by their richer fellow-citizens.

We can, with some probability, also identify some Solonian laws that explicitly recognised and regulated the lives of slaves in Attica. Some very limited protection against arbitrary homicide had probably been extended to slaves by Draco's law of homicide, a law which Solon left unchanged. The law of *hybris* covered offences against persons of any status, age or sex, and explicitly mentioned slaves as possible victims. There can be no doubt, however, that to count as *hybris* against a slave an act would have to be much more savage or gratuitously horrible than one committed against a free person. The main purpose of

Fig. 2 The padded figures on this sixth-century *symposion* scene may perhaps represent poor Athenian peasants performing comic and vulgar dances, and hoping for scraps from their rich patron's tables.

the law, after all, was to protect the status of poorer citizens, to stop them being treated as slaves. In the fourth century BC, Athenian orators found this protection for slaves remarkable, and attributed it to the 'generosity' of the Athenians, or to the concern to discourage all forms of *hybris* (Demosthenes, *Against Meidias* 21.48-50; Aeschines, *Against Timarchos* 1.15-17; cf. also below pp. 63f.).

Even if prosecutions for *hybris* or homicide against slaves rarely, if ever, occurred, it is worth noting that the laws existed, and might have had some small effect on slaveowners' behaviour. If it was indeed Solon who introduced the *hybris* law, it may be partly because he was used to slaves who were as likely to be Greek as non-Greek, and thought that the little status which a slave could be supposed to have deserved some legal consideration. Partly, also, he may have regarded slaves as part of their master's household, whose honour too might be affected by another man's gratuitously degrading or violent treatment of *his* slave, for example, by a rape or a beating at a *symposion*.

In other laws too Solon was evidently concerned to draw status-distinctions between free and slave. Slaves were not permitted to exercise naked in the wrestling grounds, to act as 'lovers' of free-born youths, or abuse their position as *paidagogoi* (attendants of boys); see Aeschines, 1.10, 138-9. They were thus excluded from anything approaching an active or equal role in the dominant social settings of their aristocratic masters, while being, as ever, commonly expected to serve the sexual demands of their masters (cf. also below pp. 62, 75, 106-7.).

Thus the notable advance for citizens represented by Solon's laws, giving them greater economic stability, a sharper definition of citizen status, and more opportunities for political participation, involved a careful differentiation between the statuses of slave and free. Can we specify more precisely a causal connection between, on the one hand, the liberation of the Athenian peasant-citizen and the gradual development of genuine citizen democracy at Athens from Solon to Pericles, and, on the other hand, the increasing use of imported chattel slaves in agriculture and other areas of the Athenian economy? A phrase of M.I. Finley's is often quoted: 'One aspect of Greek history, in short, is the advance, hand in hand, of freedom *and* slavery'; but it can be interpreted in more than one way.

To begin with, it seems likely that the progress towards democracy and the related liberation of citizens from economic exploitation by other citizens helped to encourage those with sufficient wealth to import more slaves, to work in agriculture and, increasingly in the late sixth and fifth centuries, in other areas such as manufacturing and mining (this will be discussed more fully in ch. 4). An alternative source of vulnerable labour – chattel slaves – was increasingly available in place of that of poor citizens who were now protected by the laws. Secondly, one may be tempted to take the argument a little further and say that Solon's reforms were accepted without bloodshed by the Athenians because of the existence of chattel slaves as alternative labour. This would involve supposing that the rich landowners – many of whom stayed rich and politically influential – accepted some loss of wealth and some loss of rights over some estates, partly at least because they were already aware that imported slave-labour, and perhaps also some hired free labour at peak periods, would enable them to make an acceptable surplus from their remaining land. This argument must remain no more than a speculation; it depends on one's assessment of how much land or dues individual rich men lost by the reforms, and how fast the market in imported slaves was growing.

Thirdly, the increased use of chattel slaves continued to have a major effect on the political ideology of the free. The central distinction between slave and free played an important part in the increasingly precise definition of the idea of the citizen. The initial distinction between citizen and slave was evidently made in Solon's laws; though precisely how access to citizen status was regulated at that time is very obscure. This was followed, after a period of partially controlled immigration into Attica, by Cleisthenes' reforms (508/7). These defined citizenship in terms of the new structure of demes, trittyes and tribes (as well as of the probably older organisations called phratries), and created a new status of permanent 'resident aliens' – metics – for those free people who settled in Attica. Central to this conception of the free citizen were four elements: possession of a household and an independent living (typically a farm), such that one did not work directly for another (as slaves did); freedom from regular direct taxation by the city (as was imposed on metics); the obligation to fight for the city if required (unlike women and slaves); and the right to active participation in its government, above all in its decision-making assembly and its law courts (from which slaves, metics and women were all excluded). In these elements, then, free adult male citizens were distinguished from slaves, foreigners and women; and thus the need to maintain a distinction between citizen and slave can be seen to be of increasingly paramount importance to the ordinary Athenian (cf. also ch. 8 below).

Other poleis – especially Chios
It is hard to determine how far similar processes operated in different city-states that also developed the widespread use of chattel slaves during this period. There are some hints that suggest an increased use of slaves in archaic cities such as Corinth, Samos or Cyzikos. The most interesting case is that of the island of Chios. The earliest surviving historical account of the origins of chattel slaves in Greece comes in a passage from the fourth-century historian Theopompos, quoted in the course of Athenaeus' discussion of slavery (265b-c = *GARS* 80, p. 84). This makes a reasonably clear distinction between the dependence of the serf or helot type, where a previous population has been conquered, and chattel slaves, who are bought on the market: the serfs tend to be Greek, the chattel slaves non-Greek; the serf-type is the older, chattel slavery is newer; and Chios was the first *polis* to employ chattel slavery on a large scale.

This passage raises various questions. Obviously to pick on one city as 'the first' is hopelessly overschematic and ignores chattel slaves in the Dark Ages; but it may yet reflect a dim consciousness of a considerable growth in chattel slavery in the late archaic period, and a sense that Chios was particularly involved in this process. Chios was a large and prosperous island that became known especially for its wine-exports and overseas trading; perhaps an emphasis on wine-growing rather than mixed farming encouraged greater use of slave-labour. Thucydides (8.40) commented that it had more slaves than any other Greek state except for Sparta (cf. too the report of a major agricultural slave-revolt there, discussed in ch. 6). An early sixth-century inscription suggests that Chios, like Athens, may have been experiencing significant political change. It mentions 'demarchs', and a *boule demosie* (translation available in Fornara, *Archaic Times to the end of the Peloponnesian War* [Cambridge, 1983] no. 19). This may indicate a council representing the people as a whole, as opposed to an older aristocratic council, or more probably a council of the community as a whole, as opposed to local bodies. The council had powers to fine magistrates and hear appeals. Chios, then, was a *polis* which in the archaic period saw increased use of chattel slaves, above all for the production of export-crops, and also saw some limited development towards wider political participation. In the fifth century (at least down to the later years of the Peloponnesian War) Chios appears to have enjoyed a stable regime in which rich landowners dominated the council, and a popular assembly had the final say. We cannot reconstruct the details, but our hints give some support to the possibility of a slightly different type of 'advance, hand in hand, of freedom and slavery', in which the rich exploited slave-labour rather than citizen, left citizens largely alone, and played a more prominent part in a moderate constitution than their counterparts in democratic Athens. Exactly which pattern of interlocking processes took place in those other *poleis* which developed extensive chattel slavery is not easy to unearth.

Chapter 3

Community Slaves or Serfs:
the Spartan Helots and Others

[Note: in this chapter *SL* A 1 (etc.) refers to a source translated in Appendix 4 of Paul Cartledge's *Sparta and Laconia* (London, 1979), which provides a collection of translated ancient sources on the helots.]

By the middle of the fourth century Greek writers made explicit the distinction between the bought, largely non-Greek, chattel slaves of many Greek cities and the large-scale dependent labour-forces found in a specific group of cities or regions (Sparta, Thessaly, Crete, Heraclea on the Black Sea, Syracuse and a few others). We find the distinction in Theopompos (*SL* B 5, quoted in the last chapter, and in Aristotle [see *SL* C 7] and also *GARS* 80, pp. 80-2); it is spelled out fully in the following passage from Plato, though his terminology remains slightly confusing:

> The helot-system of the Spartans, of all Greek institutions, would seem just about to provide the most intractable and contentious subject of all, as some think it was a good idea, and others that it was not; the slave-system of the Mariandynoi at Heraclea provides less dispute about the enslavement, as does also the race of Penestai in Thessaly.
>
> (Plato, *Laws* 776c-d = *SL* A 2)

A later scholar, in the Hellenistic period, loosely classified the non-chattel slaves as 'between free people and slaves (*douloi*)' (Aristophanes of Byzantium, quoted by Pollux, *Onomastikon* 3.83 = *SL* C 13). What differentiated such types of dependent labour from chattel slaves were some or all of the following: they were identifiable and cohesive populations who had been enslaved *en bloc* by conquest and forced to work for their conquerors in what they might still consider 'their' country; they were usually therefore Greek, not foreign; they tended to be the property of the city as a whole, not just owned by individuals – hence some scholars (such as Garlan in his *Slavery in Classical Greece* ch. 2), prefer to classify them as 'community slaves'; they were essentially tied to the

22

land and to particular estates, and hence were not (normally) expected to perform a wide range of different jobs or tasks for their masters, or be sold away from the estate; they were a self-reproducing group, and hence were permitted to marry and form lasting family groups and households, whether on the estate or in villages. If weight is put on these last two factors, one may, as with many scholars (e.g., de Ste. Croix in his *Class Struggle*), find it helpful to classify most of these groups as 'state-serfs' (cf. the discussion above p. 4).

Spartan helots: origins, developments and functions

Reconstructing Spartan history and society is not easy. We have no genuine Spartan sources; the Spartans themselves seem to have been masters of secrecy and propaganda; and most of our writers, many of them Athenian, have been influenced, for or against Sparta, by the debate generated by her peculiar institutions and her apparent success and stability. It is even more difficult to recover any sort of narrative of the origins of the Spartan state and of her subject-classes. What survives of the traditions of Spartan and Messenian history is seriously confused – and badly slanted – by later propaganda for or against the Spartans.

Perhaps some time after 950 BC what was to emerge as the dominant group in the southern Peloponnese, a population of Doric-Greek speakers, become established at Sparta. They were probably a group of immigrant 'Dorians' from North-West Greece, attracted by the potential for cereal crops and olive-growing afforded by the lower Eurotas valley. They then achieved dominance over this central part of the southern Peloponnese, and reduced the other populations to one of two sharply distinct types of subjection. Some became 'helots', state-serfs, forcibly attached to particular estates. Two explanations of the term were found in the ancient sources, and both make some sense in this context: either 'captives' (*heilotes*), reflecting the fact of reduction through conquest, or 'people from Helos', a region in the lower Eurotas valley which may have been one centre of the initial conquests (cf. sources in *SL* B). Other peoples became the *perioikoi*, the 'livers-around', peasants, fishermen, craftsmen, miners and traders, who led relatively free lives in their small towns and villages (and, in time, came to own chattel slaves of their own). However, they had no political independence, and were expected to serve in Sparta's armed forces with no share in making its policies.

In the eighth century BC, perhaps under pressure of over-population, the Spartans invaded Messenia, the region to the west of the

Taygetos massif dominated by the larger and more fertile valley of the Pamisos. It took a long initial war and a major revolt and war in the mid-seventh century before the conquest was complete. The Messenians thus reduced to helot-status were considerably more numerous than the Laconian helots (cf. Thucydides, 1.101); and they retained their national identity and desire for independence much more vigorously over the next four centuries. Some Messenian communities, largely outside the wealthiest valley lands, acquired perioikic status.

These conquests made Sparta more powerful, and from the beginning of the sixth century, after a failed attempt to extend the helot-system to Tegea in Arcadia, she built up a position at the head of a system of alliances that created a lasting hegemony for her in the Peloponnese (called by modern historians the Peloponnesian League). Spartan citizens ('Spartiates') became individually richer as the new Messenian lands were assigned to them as the ruling class. But this system of dependent labour created also the conditions of insecurity and permanent threat that forced the Spartans to transform most aspects of their state. These changes, which led to the creation of the classical Spartan economic, political and social systems, were attributed by most Greek authors (from Herodotus, 1.65ff. on) to a single lawgiver called Lycurgos, whose life they placed at various dates in the distant past, and to whom they attributed the sudden and lasting creation of 'good government' (*eunomia*) in place of civil discord. We should see Lycurgos as a 'useful myth' created by the Spartans, seeking to give a sense of antiquity and solidity to their complex and bizarre system. In fact, varied patterns of interlocking changes must have been adopted over a period of a hundred or more years from the early seventh century on. The single most important reason underlying all these changes was probably the perceived need to maintain control over a very large, and to a great extent permanently disaffected and cohesive, labour force, the helots, and above all the Messenian helots. The result was that Sparta became more and more like an 'armed camp' of its citizens (as many ancient writers observed, for example, Plato, *Laws* 666e and Plutarch, *Lycurgos* 24): or, in de Ste. Croix's potent image, like Fafner in Wagner's *Ring*, a giant who turned himself into a dragon, living gloomily in a cave, in order to be better able to guard the treasure of the Rhinemaidens. In the sense that they had been able to remove themselves completely from the need to perform any productive labour, the Spartiates were, as their Athenian admirer Critias said, 'the most free of all the Greeks', as the helots were 'the most enslaved' (*SL* C 1); but in the self-imposed discipline and homogeneity of their lives and culture such 'freedom' might seem intolerably constricting and repressive.

The relative numbers of helots and Spartiates cannot be known with any accuracy, but we can be sure that they entailed a large-scale problem of control, and that this increased very considerably from the mid-fifth century BC on. During the Persian Wars, Sparta could put 5,000 Spartiate hoplites and 5,000 *periokoi* into the last decisive battle at Plataea in 479 BC (Herodotus, 9.28-9), and probably had about 8,000 male Spartiates in all at that time (Herodotus, 7.234). A decline in Spartiate manpower set in soon after, though its pace and causes are matters of great dispute that cannot be discussed here. At the equally decisive battle of Leuctra (371 BC) they put a mere 700 into the field, of whom 400 were killed (Xenophon, *History of Greece* 6.4.15-17), and the total number of Spartiates seems to have been between 1,000 and 1,500 (cf. Aristotle, *Politics* 1270a29-32). At the time of the Peloponnesian War, the best guess is that there were about 3,000 Spartiates. How much of this steep decline was the result of the possibly massive losses sustained during the severe earthquake of the mid-460s, and how much of long-term tensions and contradictions in the operations of her systems of inheritance, property-regulation and citizenship, remains controversial. (For what I think are the most plausible explanations, see the works by Cartledge and Hodkinson listed in the bibliography.)

For the helots, the only figure comes also from Herodotus' Plataea narrative; seven helots, he repeatedly claims, accompanied each of the 5,000 Spartiates. One may doubt that it was thought necessary or desirable to let as many as 35,000 helots out on campaign, but the figure may reflect a general opinion that there were roughly seven times as many helots as Spartiates; if so, one must ask what such an opinion would be based on, and how keen the Spartans would be to let true figures (if they had them) be widely known. It is safer to accept the general perception that the helot class was larger than any other slave-class in Greece, as Thucydides claims (8.40 and also 4.80), that helots outnumbered Spartiates by a considerable factor, and that this factor was increasing rapidly from the Persian Wars onwards.

The main function of the helots was to perform agricultural labour on the estates to which they were tied. They were also, as we have just seen, used as light-armed troops, attendants and supply-labour on campaigns and increasingly, as the Spartiate population declined, in more active capacities in war. Helots were also used as domestic servants and as cooks, waiters and so on in the common messes. Helots were attached to particular estates (*klaroi*), and could only be killed, released or transferred from their estates, or set free, by order of the state. In that sense they were, as the first-century Greek geographer Strabo puts it (8.4.5 = *SL* C 11), 'in some way public slaves'. In another way, as Strabo's wording implies, they 'belonged' to those individual Spartan citizens on whose estates they worked and to whom they paid their 'rent' in kind. According to Tyrtaeus, the mid-seventh century Spartan poet, they paid them half their produce (fr. 6 = *SL* D 1 = *GARS* 15), but we do not know if the proportion was still the same during the classical period. Their individual masters were responsible for supervising the helots' work and ensuring their good behaviour. The political and economic status of these masters depended on the production of their helots, since citizenship was conditional on individual Spartiates maintaining a certain level of contributions, in the form of produce, to their 'common messes' (*syssitia*); this pressure to produce would of course be transferred to the helots.

But the use, management and control of all helots was recognised as a joint responsibility of all Spartiates. As they enjoyed an allegedly 'equal' life-style, they could all in theory make casual use of each other's helots, as of their dogs or horses (Xenophon, *Spartan Society* 6). No Spartiate was permitted (under pain of a 'public curse') to exact more than the accepted proportion of crops in rent (*SL* F 2.b), so as to prevent too much pressure being applied to the helots. In particular, Spartans had always to remember that the helots were their conquered enemies who might rise in revolt at any time, and for that reason, it seems, every year 'the ephors, as soon as they first enter into their office, declare war on the helots, so that it may be religiously proper to do away with them' (Plutarch, *Lycurgos* 28, quoting Aristotle). Thus we see that not only is it a plausible mode of analysis to classify the Spartiate/helot relationship as a 'class-war', in that the Spartan economic system and its wealth depended above all on the forced labour of the helots, who sought constantly to break free; it is actually recognised as an open and permanent war by the ruling class itself, though the apparent reason for this frankness was a narrow religious scruple – to avoid the religious 'pollution' of unjustified killing.

Control of the helots: terror, division, encouragement and confusion

Two celebrated passages reveal graphically how the Spartans exercised the right they gave themselves to treat the killing of helots as legitimate acts of state. First, there is an incident recorded by Thucydides. During the Peloponnesian War, in 425, the Athenians had captured the headland of Pylos in Messenian territory, had captured 120 Spartiate prisoners on the island of Sphacteria, and were beginning to encourage neighbouring helots to join them in revolt. Thucydides reports that at that time the Spartans were so afraid of the hostility and numbers of the helots that they devised the following plan:

> Most Spartan institutions in relation to the helots have always been organised with a view to security. They made a proclamation to them to choose those of their number who claimed to have proved themselves excellent fighters for the Spartans in the wars, as they (the Spartans) were going to set them free; they did this as a test, thinking that those who claimed themselves to be the most worthy of being set free would also be those possessing the greatest spirit to attack them. When they had selected up to 2,000, those helots put garlands on their heads and went around the shrines as if they had been set free, but the Spartans, not long afterwards, made them disappear, and no one found out by what means each of them was destroyed.
>
> (Thucydides, 4.80 = *SL* D 5)

Such a spectacular and well-organised fraud and massacre was a remarkable feat of devious and intelligent organisation on the part of the Spartan authorities. Apparently up to 2,000 men, selected for their boldness and courage, were coldly deceived and then murdered, by the secretive officials and their selected nocturnal killers, who belonged to the ruling class of Spartiate citizen-soldiers, numbering, as mentioned above, perhaps only c. 3,000 in all. The great nineteenth-century historian George Grote judged that 'this strategem at once so perfidious in the contrivance, so murderous in the purpose, and so complete in the execution, stands without parallel in any history'; one may argue whether or not twentieth-century outrages surpassed it. Thucydides' account should probably be accepted as essentially correct, though one could wish that he had indicated more precisely when he thought it took place, and from what sources he had learnt of the event. Thucydides himself comments on the secretiveness of the Spartan state and the difficulty of discovering accurate information about her affairs or the numbers in her army (5.68), but he is not so hostile to Sparta that he is likely to have invented such a story or accepted it without reason.

Killing on such a huge scale could not have occurred very often, without destroying the economy as well as the prospect of any trust between Spartans and helots. It reveals the anxiety Spartans were beginning to feel about the extent to which they were outnumbered, and the justified fear that the Athenian presence at Pylos might stir a large-scale revolt (cf. also Thucydides, 4.41). Thucydides, however, goes on in the same chapter (4.80) to describe how the Spartans, apparently within a year, sent out a force of 700 helots with their commander Brasidas, and how the survivors were later freed, and then served the Spartans as a garrison in Elis (Thucydides, 5.34). These facts show the complexity of Spartan treatment of their helots; they were extremely adept at combining, in confusing ways, false carrots, very big sticks, and the occasional real carrot.

But small-scale helot-killing seems to have been a matter of some regularity. Herodotus mentions that Spartans carried out all their killings 'by night' (4.146); and Plutarch, basing himself again on Aristotle's lost *Constitution of the Spartans*, gives a detailed account of a special Spartan institution:

> In all of this (i.e. the measures Plutarch has just been describing) there is no sign of the injustice and excess for which some find fault with Lycurgos' laws, arguing that they make sufficient provision for courage, but are lacking in justice. The so-called *krypteia* ('secret operation') of theirs, if it really was one of Lycurgos' institutions, may be what led Plato as well to that opinion about the system and the man. It operated like this: the leaders of the young men from time to time would send out those who seemed to have the most sense into the countryside in different directions, equipped with daggers and sufficient provisions, but nothing else; by day they made their way in scattered groups to remote places and hid themselves and rested; at night they came down into the roads and slaughtered any of the helots they caught. Often too they journeyed into the fields and did away with the strongest and bravest of them.
>
> (Plutarch, *Lycurgos* 28 = *SL* D 6)

Plato, in his *Laws*, while making some serious criticisms of Sparta, presented a much more favourable (or 'sanitised') picture of the *krypteia*, emphasising its role in training young Spartans in endurance – ranging over the whole country in winter, night and day, barefoot, without bedclothes, and without attendants (633c). Plutarch accepted the helot-killing version as a reality, but preferred the view that it, and other aspects of savage or degrading treatment, only took root after a crisis in Spartan-helot relations brought on by the earthquake of the 460s. Aristotle, who was in general much more systematically critical of Sparta than his teacher Plato, seems to have seen its faults and eventual decline in the fourth century in terms of the structural tensions and errors built into the 'Lycurgan' system, and hence did not see the *krypteia* and its established cruelty as a recent development. The account in Plutarch, it must be noted, does not make it clear how often this operation took place (every month? annually at fixed times? or only when a need was felt by the authorities?); nor does it give any idea how many helots might be 'culled' in this way.

We need to distinguish clearly between the origins of this institution and its operation as part of the system of helot-control. As was first pointed out by the French scholar H. Jeanmaire in 1913, using ethnographic parallels from Africa, the picture of young men about to become adults and soldiers, ranging about in the remote countryside, operating by night, by deceit, on their own, and with the lightest of arms, strongly suggests an origin in the last phase of boys' initiation rituals into manhood. In such rituals youths in a transitional or 'liminal' stage act out a role-reversal of the norms of adult male society – in the Greek case the norms of the cohesive, heavily-armed, hoplite infantry. Parallels in the shadowy records of other Greek cities suggest that such initiation rituals had existed, but usually then decayed or were transformed to suit the needs of growing *poleis* (this theme has been well explored by another French historian, P. Vidal-Naquet). Such initiation rituals often involve – in Greece and elsewhere – homosexual pair-bondings, which are in fact well attested in the developed upbringing-system for young Spartiates, and also the hunting of animals on foot and with nets in the wild country.

But the Spartan *krypteia* described by Plutarch is a systematic and deliberate re-institutionalisation of such rituals for the purpose of controlling and creating terror among the helots, who become the victims of the 'hunt'. His description also suggests two distinct modes of operation: firstly, the nocturnal and murderous supervision of a *de facto* curfew on helots moving on the roads (which would be intended to inhibit organised resistance, brigandage or flight); and secondly, the selective killing, presumably after tip-offs had been received, of potentially dangerous individuals. Just how initiatory endurance and hunting became systematic state-terror remains as uncertain as does the actual extent of the killing. Most scholars now believe that a major re-organisation of the Spartan system of boys' upbringing (the *agoge*) took place around the time of the Second Messenian War or in the following century (c. 650-550). This involved the re-institutionalisation and adaptation of old initiation rituals into a disciplined and highly hierarchical structure of 'age-classes' and military and political training to suit Sparta's needs. Some scholars, though, are tempted to follow the line suggested by Plutarch and suppose that regular, officially-organised killing of helots rather than animals only began after the earthquake and the Messenian Revolt of the 460s, which produced an awareness of a growing numerical disparity. Some are even inclined to treat it as a matter of ritualistic or symbolic behaviour, that would reinforce for the helots the huge gulf between them and Spartiates, without involving (much) actual killing. Others (and I would tend to agree with them) suppose that helot-killing too went back to the earlier re-organisation of the system of upbringing, though some intensification of it may well have occurred from the mid-fifth century on. Overall, while few would now follow Plato in (implicitly) denying any secret helot-killing by the Spartan youths, there is room for considerable disagreement on just how pervasive an operation it was.

Many other indications of systematic maltreatment are given in our sources: degradation, demoralisation and reminders of permanent inferiority seem to be the main objectives of these practices. According to a Messenian history by a third-century BC historian, Myron of Priene (a source probably biased in favour of the Messenians), helots had to wear distinctive, and inferior, clothing – rustic animal skin caps and clothes – and be subjected to regular beatings even if they had done no wrong, 'so that they should never forget that they were slaves' (*SL* D 7). According to the same chapter in Plutarch's *Lycurgos* quoted above, Spartans would make individual helots drunk on unmixed wine and bring them into the Spartiates' common messes. They would also force them to perform vulgar and silly dances and songs, while not permitting them to sing the songs which Spartiates used to sing; this may have occurred at the common messes, or at specific religious festivals, or perhaps at both. Helots were thus encouraged or forced to play the roles, as buffoons and vulgar dancers, that were performed in other places by poor clients, parasites, and slave or foreign entertainers. In Plutarch's view, in addition to the harshness involved, the purpose was to instil in Spartiates a sense of 'what drunkenness was like'. This is a plausible idea, since in the interests of collective cohesion and an equally austere life-style for all the 'Equals', the system clearly sought to prevent the sort of regular male drinking sessions which were tolerated in other states.

It is likely that the effects of these practices would be confusing, and were intended to be so. Being selected for an evening's merrymaking might seem a privilege in relation to other helots, even though the helots were themselves being humiliated. Spartans made considerable efforts to separate helots from one another by giving some of them superior functions as supervisors in the fields, in domestic duties, or in rituals; in general they also sought to persuade helots to accept and to internalise the social and political gulf between themselves and their masters. There is evidence for believing that this policy had some success, particularly with the Laconian helots. Even when the Thebans invaded Laconia in 370 BC, it was only the Messenians who revolted successfully. Large numbers of Laconian helots accepted the offer of enlistment with the Spartans (1,000 according to Diodoros, 6,000 according to Xenophon), and some captured helots refused to sing the Spartiates' chief songs, saying their masters would not like it (Plutarch, *Lycurgos* 28).

Perhaps the chief spur to loyalty was the hope of some sort of freedom, as with chattel slavery elsewhere. It seems likely that the frequency of manumission of helots increased, as did the methods of inspiring fear, precisely as the numerical disparity grew. Sparta appears to have deployed a baffling number and variety of terms for those granted apparently different levels of privilege. According to Myron of Priene there were those called *aphetai* ('released'), *adespotai* ('masterless'), *erykteres* ('restrainers') and *desposionautai* ('master-seamen'), and we hear most of all about those called *neodamodeis* ('new members of the demos'), like the survivors of Brasidas' army mentioned above (*SL* C 8, Thucydides, 5.34). Despite their title, these last did not become Spartiates (any more than freed slaves in Athens or elsewhere in Greece became citizens); but they served as hoplites in the army and were used as garrisons on the frontiers. These groups of ex-helots were presumably freed above all from the harsh conditions of labour-dues. In addition, there was at Sparta a growing number of status-groups in decline, including bastard children of Spartiates and helot-women (*mothakes*), and those demoted through cowardice, failure to maintain the mess-payments of produce, or because of incompetence in the *agoge* – generally known as the *hypomeiones* ('Inferiors'). Thus the principle of 'Divide and Rule' was operated with considerable ingenuity, and the system doubtless kept individuals in these intermediate statuses more or less docile as a result of many individual acts of patronage (such as meals at the messes). On the other hand, the more members of the lower status-groups might be singled out for privilege or advancement, the more (if they were wise), they might fear sudden removal.

A final story told by Xenophon, perhaps somewhat over-dramatised, rounds off these themes. In c. 397 BC a brave young 'Inferior' called Cinadon, who claimed later under torture that he had wanted to be 'lesser to no one in Sparta', planned a revolt. He encouraged potential conspirators by pointing out how, among those present in the Spartan civic centre, the Spartiates were outnumbered roughly 100:1 by those belonging to the lesser status-groups – and Xenophon's account names the four chief ones: helots, *neodamodeis, hypomeiones* and *perioikoi*. All of these, according to Cinadon, would 'gladly eat the Spartiates raw'. An informer gave away the incipient plot, and the Spartan ephors, with a few of the Council of Elders (the *Gerousia*), devised highly cunning counter-moves. Making use of the fact that Cinadon had already been employed in secret manoeuvres with 'the young men' (the *krypteia*, presumably), they arranged to have him arrested far away from the city and tortured to reveal his fellow-conspirators (Xenophon, *History of Greece* 3.3.4-11).

In the end, despite the large-scale revolts in the mid-seventh and the mid-fifth centuries, and mini-revolts like Cinadon's, efficiently and ruthlessly crushed, and despite the growing evidence of tensions within the system and the disastrous failure of the ruling class to reproduce itself, it took military defeat and an invasion of Laconia by the Thebans in 371-0 BC to achieve the permanent liberation of the Messenian helots (but not of the Laconian), and a lasting end to Sparta's position of hegemony in the Greek world. The more Spartan economic, social and political systems can be seen to be collapsing under a network of internal tensions and contradictions, the more remarkable becomes the discipline, organisation and subtlety with which her rulers, so few in number, maintained their physical and ideological grip over their serfs. The need was indeed great: the helots were the ultimate source of their wealth and power, and in all probability the chief cause of their having adopted for themselves such an austere, and ultimately unsustainable, life-style.

Serf-systems in other states

Very much less is known about other serfs. On the island of Crete the various city-states had systems that were frequently compared to Sparta's. According to our literary sources, which are basically fourth-century political theorists and historians such as Plato, Aristotle and Ephoros, the Cretan political systems were geared for war, though less intensively than the Spartan, and enjoyed considerable stability. There was a male citizen class that maintained the observance of regular collective dining in 'messes', and some initiatory homosexual educational practices. There was also a complex variety of dependent, largely agrarian, status-groups: some, though free, lacked citizenship, and thus resembled the *perioikoi*; some appear to have been serfs, tied to the land,

and called *Mnoitai*, or *Klarotai*; and some look more like chattel slaves, though evidently with rather more legal privileges than those in Athens. But we remain almost entirely in the dark as to how the systems worked: how we are to marry our generalised literary accounts with the detailed extracts from the one law-code which has survived on stone (from Gortyn); how much those systems changed over time or varied from one city in Crete to another; or why they seem to have caused much less discontent than in Sparta. Aristotle's explanation for this last question was that neighbouring cities never supported each other's subject groups in revolt even when they were at war with them, and that Crete stayed isolated from Greece's wars (*Politics* 1269a39-b2, 1272b16-22).

The other large-scale group of this serf type on the Greek mainland, the *Penestai* in Thessaly, were, like the helots, in all probability defeated inhabitants of the region who were forced to work on fixed conditions on their lands, but may have been given some protection from being exported or killed by their landlords (according to an author quoted by Athenaeus, 264 = *GARS* 80, p. 82). According to Aristotle (*Politics* 1269a35-9) they did give more trouble, and according to the same Athenaeus extract (from an author later than Aristotle, though his precise date is unclear) some of them became richer than their masters. Inasmuch as Thessaly was a less cohesive aristocratic state, her serfs were probably less tightly controlled and oppressed than Sparta's helots. Elsewhere, we hear of varied and colourfully titled subordinate groupings in some other Peloponnesian cities, such as the 'club-wearers' or 'sheepskin-wearers' at Sicyon, the 'dusty-feet' at Epidauros or the 'Naked Ones' at Argos; and – what are probably only a few tips of a large number of nasty icebergs – in the places the Greeks colonized we hear of subordinate serf-type groups in Syracuse called the Kallikyrioi, in Heraclea on the Black Sea called the Mariandynoi, and in Byzantium we hear of groups of Bithynians (cf. *GARS* 80, pp. 88-9, *SL* B.5, 9; C.7). How important these labour-groups were in their respective cities remains obscure (but probably not to be under-estimated). A recurring pattern of stories from the middle of the fourth century BC suggest that such disgruntled groups provided a constant source of support for allegedly radical rulers such as Dionysius I in Syracuse, Clearchos in Heraclea, and Euphron in Sicyon, whom our generally conservative-minded sources regard with deep hostility and label as tyrants. The same fate was to befall those Spartan kings in the late third and early second century BC (Agis IV, Cleomenes III and Nabis) who attempted to bring back some glory to Sparta by reforming the land-tenure system and 'liberating' some of the *perioikoi* or helots.

Chapter 4
Slaves in Classical Athens: Numbers, Origins and Economic Functions

Athens, the most prosperous and one of the two most powerful of Greek *poleis* in the fifth century BC, was remarkable above all for its stable peasant-citizen democracy, and for its varied and influential cultural achievements. This chapter looks at the importance of chattel slavery in the Athenian economy; chapter 8 will explore also the effects it had on the attitudes of Athenian citizens towards all aspects of their work and leisure. The precise degree of Athens' economic dependence on slavery, and hence the relationship between its democracy and slavery, are matters of great dispute. The dispute focuses on the extent to which slaves were used on the farms from which most Athenians gained their livelihoods.

Numbers of slaves

Chattel slavery began to be important in Athens at the time of Solon's reforms, or soon afterwards (cf. ch. 2 above); it became markedly more significant through the fifth century as Athens developed her democracy, and her victories over the Persians and the growth of the Athenian Empire brought unparalleled collective and individual wealth to the new dominant state in the Aegean world. We have no usable figures for the numbers of slaves in Athens or, for that matter, anywhere else in Greece, at any period. In Athenaeus' discussion of slavery (272b-c = *GARS* p. 90) we do find three figures, which he took from three different authors. He found a figure for Corinth of 460,000 slaves in Timaios, the early third-century BC historian. For Athens, he claims that Ctesicles, another Hellenistic historian, who based his figures allegedly on the census of Demetrios of Phaleron taken c. 310 BC, gave figures of 21,000 adult male Athenian citizens, 10,000 metics, and 400,000 slaves. For Aegina, Athenaeus found a figure of 470,000 slaves in Aristotle's *Constitution of the Aeginetans*. All these figures for slaves are totally unconvincing. Firstly, they imply impossibly high population densities for the states concerned; secondly, there is no reason to believe that any state ever actually held a census of their slaves, as they did of their citizens or resident foreigners, for example, for military purposes (hence the figures for citizens and metics in Athens in this passage are much more likely to be accurate). The slavery figures can only be the wildest of guesses, from which we can conclude two things. First, those three cities were thought to have unusually large chattel slave populations and second, Greeks were inclined to exaggerate hugely the numbers of slaves in a state. It seems most likely that Athens was the biggest slave-society, and Corinth, Aegina and also Chios had large numbers of slaves. Aegina and Corinth seem especially to have developed trading and manufacturing interests as well as agriculture, whereas Chiot slaves seem to have worked mostly in agriculture and viticulture. Of these states, we may note that Athens was a democracy for a long period, Chios alternated between different types of regimes, while Corinth and Aegina were broadly-based oligarchies. Thus we can see that the conjunction of freedom and a high development of chattel slavery is compatible with rule by moderate oligarchs, who used slaves extensively and perhaps left their peasants alone.

One other figure for Athenian slaves is slightly less absurd. The Athenian politician Hypereides proposed, in the desperate crisis after the defeat at Chaeronea in 338 BC, that the slaves 'from the mines and throughout the countryside, who were more than 150,000', metics and the disenfranchised be all enlisted to fight; the proposal was defeated (Hypereides, fr. 29 = GARS 89). The figure was at best an educated guess, and probably a greatly exaggerated one. We are a little better off with figures for Athenian male citizens, where c. 30,000 seems a plausible average figure for most of the fourth century, and c. 45,000 a maximum at the height of Athenian prosperity before the Peloponnnesian War. For numbers of adult metics in Athens, the c. 310 BC census figure of c. 10,000 had very likely been exceeded in earlier, more prosperous times, when the citizen population had also been higher.

For slave numbers in Athens we are therefore reduced to speculation, based on estimates of their economic and social importance. At the outset one may note that estimates varying from the very low c. 20,000 slaves, through moderate ones of c. 50,000-60,000, up to high ones like c. 100,000-120,000, all have supporters, and decision between these limits is not easy. Slave numbers too would obviously have varied at different times, as did those of the other categories, depending both on the numbers and the wealth of the potential slaveowners. Cautiously, one may suggest that slaves may have made up anything between c. 15% to c. 35% of the total population, depending on which of the estimates one accepts. The lower figures are still sufficient to classify Athens as a slave-society, but whether in a stronger or a weaker sense depends on which estimates one prefers and, more importantly, on what economic functions the slaves performed.

The sources of slaves

After Solon's reforms, Athenians could not be enslaved in Athens (there were a very few, and no doubt very rare, exceptions, such as sexually offending daughters enslaved by fathers, who were probably in any case sold to be slaves outside Athens). Other Greeks might be enslaved as a result of a savage decision of the victors in wars (for example, the Athenians enslaved the wives and children of the Melians and some others of their subject cities who had rebelled during the Peloponnesian War), or as a result of brigandage or piracy. Such enslavements were often temporary. In the latter case, many might be ransomed back into freedom by relatives or friends, often using the mechanism of raising an interest-free loan (*eranos*). Good examples of Athenians thus restored are found in two speeches in the Demosthenic collection, 53.6-9, and 58.18-19. (Ransomed ex-slaves who failed to pay back the loan raised could become the slaves of the ransomer.) The city concerned might also encourage individuals by financial inducements and other honours to find and ransom their enslaved fellow-citizens. In the former case, where the city had been 'destroyed', it was often restored again in changed political circumstances; enslaved members might then be found and brought home, as happened in the cases of both Plataea and Melos in the fourth century. Some infants of Greek birth may have been exposed because of their parents' poverty or because they were unwanted bastards, and then found and sold to be slaves. How often this happened is unknown; but the chances of any such slaves being 'recognised' by their original families and restored to freedom were minimal, despite the prevalence of this pattern in the plots of Greek plays.

Our sources give the impression that virtually all chattel slaves in Athens were of non-Greek ('barbarian') origin. This may be exaggerated. In the late fifth and the fourth centuries BC the ideological belief in the 'natural' slavery of the barbarian grew, and moral doubts about the legitimacy of enslaving other Greeks also increased, and as a result Greek writers would probably tend to suppress mention of those Greek slaves who did exist. Even so, in practice the majority of slaves in Athens probably were non-Greek. Three mechanisms providing foreign slaves for slave-traders and markets can be distinguished: wars, piracy, and direct trade with those 'barbarian' countries where captive, surplus or subordinate populations were regularly sold (in ways comparable to the African slave-trade to the New World). The third of these is likely to have been at least as important as the other two, and indeed was probably the most important. The traffic was carried on by specialised slave traders, who followed the armies, or dealt direct with the pirates and the non-Greek authorities. We hear very little of the activities of the slave traders, especially since the moral ambiguity of the institution and the obvious unpleasantness and dangers involved in transporting new slaves combined to make it among the most shameful of occupations (cf. Xenophon, *Symposion* 4.36: 'Through poverty some men steal, or burgle, or become slavers'). One of the best available indications of the sources of slaves is the inscription recording the sales of the property of those convicted of involvement in the Herms and Mysteries affairs of 415 BC (translated extracts can be found in Fornara, *Archaic Times* 147). This (and other evidence) suggests that among the regions regularly supplying slaves to Greek markets were Thrace and Scythia to the north-east, Caria, Phrygia and Syria to the east, Illyria in the north-west. The inscription also reveals two slaves who came from the Greek world, an expensive Macedonian woman (costing 310 drachmai), and a less expensive woman from Messene (130 drachmai): this woman was presumably either an ex-helot or came from Messene in Sicily.

The final source of new slaves was of course, breeding, whether by permitting slaves to have sex or form permanent relationships with each other as a reward, or as a result of masters' sexual exploitation of slave-women. A small proportion of 'house-bred' slaves appear in the sources for the classical period (three are found on the inscription mentioned above). Xenophon (*Oikonomikos* 9.5 = GARS 93) insists on strict supervision and locking up of slaves to prevent the bad ones from breeding, and at the same time allowing the privilege of breeding to the good ones, thereby increasing their loyalty. The Pseudo-Aristotelian *Oikonomika* (1.5 = GARS 206) adds the hard-nosed advantages that slave-children can serve as hostages for their parents' good behaviour, and can replace them when they grow up.

Slaves in agriculture: alternative views

This is the most intractable problem concerning Athenian slavery, and on it depends much of our judgement of Athenian society and democracy. Most Athenians worked as peasant-farmers with their families on small plots of land; how many of them were able to use slave-labour on

Fig. 3 Olive-pickers, on a sixth-century Attic black-figure vase. One cannot tell whether these agricultural workers are slaves or free.

their land to earn a little more wealth and to enjoy a little more leisure? One apparently statistical statement supporting the view that most Athenians owned some land may be cited, though its precise value is uncertain. When the Athenians debated what form of government should be established after the fall of the Thirty Tyrants in 403 BC, one Phormisios made the not wholly democratic proposal that only those who owned some land in Attica should be citizens. A fragment of a speech composed by Lysias for use against Phormosios' proposal (speech 34 = Dionysius

Halicarnassus, *Lysias* 32), claims that this proposal would mean that 5,000 Athenians, who owned no land, would be disenfranchised. The difficulties with this text are that it was presumably at best merely a rough estimate, and we cannot be sure what was meant by 'land' – a proper farm outside the city walls, or could merely an urban vegetable garden count? But as far it goes, it does suggests that a large majority of Athenians owned some land, even at the end of the disruptions of the Peloponnesian War (at the start of the war, according to Thucydides, 2.16, most Athenians were born and lived in the countryside of Attica).

The wealth of the rich in Athens was traditionally based on landed estates. However, the patterns of inheritance (equal division between sons) and of dowry-settlements usually produced an accumulation of individual, scattered farms rather than single large estates. This pattern operated with the smallholdings of the peasants as well as with large estates, and was believed, with reason, to represent a sensible strategy of minimising the risks of bad weather or crop-diseases, as well as being the fairest for one's children. Many influential families with landed wealth developed other interests from the fifth century on; but many of those who became wealthy in other ways would buy farms for respectability and security. Most moderately well-off or poor citizens (hoplites and thetes) had a medium-sized or small farm: such evidence as we have suggests that c. 4-6 hectares (= c. 10-15 acres) was considered then, as it is in many peasant communities now, to be the minimum necessary for a viable household.

Such smallholders should be thought of as 'peasants', provided that we also recognise that in three respects they were quite untypical and privileged peasants compared with those of other societies. Firstly, they were free both from the burdens of rents or work-duties to richer farmers and also from state taxes. Secondly, they could participate extensively in their city's politics. Thirdly, the social and moral distinctions between city and countryside was relatively undeveloped in Athens. Further, there is no good reason to suppose, as used to be thought, that peasants who lost farms or moved into the city during the troubles of the Peloponnesian War failed as a class to recover their position on the land afterwards. The extent of the damage done to the land during the war was not as great as has often been argued; and fourth-century evidence, and the very stability of the democracy itself, both suggest that many peasant-citizens remained free and independent on their farms throughout the period of the democracy.

Hence the extent to which slaves were productively employed in agriculture is crucial if we are to answer other vital questions: how far the Athenian economic system and her democracy 'depended on slavery', and how many moderate and poor Athenians were themselves slaveowners. There are perhaps two broad positions currently taken: each of these positions may be held in a more or less extreme form. The first view (here called 'minimalist') is that slavery was little used on farms in Attica. The more extreme version of this is that not even the rich made much use of slave labour in farming (though they used slaves for their domestic and leisure needs), and the poor not at all; the less extreme view admits that rich farmers employed them on some of their farms at least, though they will also have made use of temporary hired labour. The other position (here called 'maximalist') suggests that slave-labour was fairly widespread among farmers; the more extreme version of this view sees even quite poor farmers employing slaves on their small farms, while the more moderate view would claim that only the middling farmers used slave-labour.

A very important part of the argument is an assessment of the nature of agriculture in Attica. Two factors should be stressed at the start. The first is the absence of single large estates, where economies of scale might encourage large labour forces; instead, the predominance of small-sized, scattered estates in Athens was more likely to encourage large landowners to lease some or all of them to tenant farmers. The second factor is the nature of Mediterranean dry agriculture, which is strongly seasonal. Most farms would have been mixed, growing a certain amount of staple grain (wheat and barley), olives and vines, fruit trees and a variety of vegetables, with, usually, a few animals as well; it is clear that there were periods of intensive labour (such as ploughing, sowing, weeding, harvesting, vintages) and lengthy slacker periods.

The 'minimalist' view
These two factors are used by those holding this view to argue that the wealthier farmers would not manage their large farms, or their different estates, most efficiently if they relied solely on slave-labour, and also that a peasant and his family with a small farm would be unable to justify employing even one male slave if he were viewed essentially as a farm hand, and would be unlikely to make enough profit to purchase an all-purpose slave. Even so the extreme view that there was very little use of slave-labour even on large farms is, rightly, I believe, not now widely held (as it was, for example by Jones, *Athenian Democracy*). One argument against it is the picture of farming presented in Xenophon's *Oikonomikos* ('The art of Household Management'), a pamphlet written in the early fourth century, and set as Socratic conversations in the latter

years of the fifth, that prosperous and industrious land-owning gentlemen will have many farms whose work force will be largely slave, a picture which is unlikely to be wholly wrong. A more general argument would be that no one doubts that all prosperous and rich Athenians owned some slaves, as domestics and as status-symbols, and surely such landowners would have used many of their slaves for the necessary agricultural work throughout the year. This is perfectly consistent with the hiring of extra free labour at peak periods.

More plausible is the less extreme version of this 'minimalist' view, well presented recently by Wood, *Peasant-Citizen and Slave* and by Sallares, *Ecology of the Ancient Greek World*, who argue that while the richer farmers used some slave-labour, topped up with non-slave labour, and also hired free men (often metics) as tenant farmers for other of their farms, middling to small farmers would not have used slaves on the land at all, but worked farms with a combination of family labour, extra help organised with the neighbours on a reciprocal basis, and perhaps a little hired labour from the free poor (metics or citizens) with little or no land. On this view agricultural slavery existed, but was of little or no direct importance for the majority of the hoplites and thetes farming in Attica, who would be more likely to buy an ox before a slave.

The 'maximalist' view
The alternative or 'maximalist' position is that all the rich and relatively prosperous farmers had a good many slaves, and used them on their farms (some perhaps even going for specialist 'vine-dressers' and the like), and that many more ordinary farmers made some use of slave-labour. On the more moderate version of this (e.g., in Sinclair, *Democracy and Participation*) not only the rich, but also all the payers of the property tax (*eisphora*) – some 6,000 citizens – would have employed slaves on any farm(s) they had, and so too would perhaps most or all of the hoplite class, some 9,000 citizens. The fewer slaves one had, the more one would use them for a variety of tasks, productive and non-productive, i.e. they would work on the land when needed but would also accompany their masters when out, go shopping, serve at dinner, and so on. The more extreme version (held, for example, by Jameson, *Agriculture and Slavery*, Garlan, *Slavery* 60-4, and de Ste. Croix, *Class Struggle* 505-6) would extend such ownership of one or a few slaves to poorer peasants, including some at least of the *thetes* (no one believes that *all* Athenians owned at least one slave). On this view, quite small estates (of a few hectares) could be and were run in a very labour-intensive manner (for example, using elaborate terracing of hilly terrain); such

estates might, it is argued, have provided enough labour and profit to maintain one or two slaves and also, along with family labour and mutual neighbourly assistance, afford enough leisure for the peasant-citizen to participate at times in the political activities of the *polis*. One must note, however, that this view does not hold that slave-owning enabled ordinary Athenians to become men of leisure, able to devote all their lives to politics or leisure, nor that the limited amounts of payment offered for jury-service, political office-holding or military service would release them from the need for hard manual work.

The evidence
The evidence of literary texts and inscriptions, constantly debated, is insufficient to resolve this controversy. Some of the key items may be briefly discussed. Most interpreters of Xenophon's *Oikonomikos* agree that his detailed advice supposes farms managed by a slave-overseer with (relatively small) numbers of slave-workers (see, for example, chs V, IX, XII-XV); though the possibility of hiring a free tenant to manage a farm is also considered (I 3-4). Some, though (e.g., Osborne, *Demos* 144 and Wood, *Peasant-Slave* 49) suggest that in chapter V, for example, he may have free hired workers or co-operating neighbours rather, or as well, in mind. In this passage (V.14ff. = *GARS* 139), however, the emphasis is that guiding and commanding troops in an army is comparable to leading and ordering slave-agricultural workers, in that you need not only to work with them and get their support, but also to discipline the slackers; and the central point is brought out explicitly at the end – slave-workers, as well as free troops, need hopes. Thus it seems clear that here, and elsewhere, Xenophon has essentially slave-labour in mind. But since he is writing about gentleman-farming, the point does not take one very far.

Another important text is Thucydides' report that 'more than 20,000 slaves, and of these the greater part skilled workers', fled as part of the disruption suffered by the Athenian countryside during the period of Spartan occupation of the fort at Decelea in northern Attica (412-404) (7.27 = *GARS* 211). The text presents a number of problems. Thucydides cannot have acquired an accurate figure, and this can only be his best guess, arrived at after talking to Athenians who lost slaves, and perhaps to Spartans who received and dealt with the runaways (largely by selling them to Boeotians). Second, how many of these slaves were agricultural labourers, how many mining slaves, and how many craftsmen in the towns and villages of Attica? Some argue that the word 'skilled' or 'specialist' (*cheirotechnai*) points essentially to mining slaves and other artisans (e.g., Wood, Jameson, Sallares), others that it points not to miners (who would have been thought unskilled) but rather to craftsmen and skilled agricultural specialists such as vine-dressers (so de Ste. Croix). The text is thereby highly ambiguous: it suggests there were perhaps some slaves working at least some of the time in the countryside, but cannot safely be used to support either side in this controversy.

Various passages in the surviving law-court speeches give information on individual property holdings. These support the view that the predominant land-owning pattern was indeed the accumulation of separate, scattered farms, and that leasing them to tenant farmers was common. Most details of properties in such speeches concern wealthy litigants. There are some specific references to slave-workers in a farming context: e.g., Pseudo-Demosthenes, 47.52ff., slaves on the property of a rich man; Demosthenes, 55.31ff., a slave building a wall on the farm of (apparently) a relatively poor man; and Pseudo-Demosthenes, 53.6, 21, slaves on the farm of (probably) a wealthy man, some of whom may be hired out at harvest time to others. On the other hand the inventories of land in such speeches or in lists of sales on inscriptions merely state the units (*plethra*) of land, but do not indicate numbers of slaves, whereas itemised 'factories' of craftsmen do list slaves (an example: Aeschines, 1.97 = *GARS* 91). But this essentially reflects the fact that in manufacturing slaves *were* the business – they were skilled artisans, and there was little in the way of machinery involved – whereas slaves who worked primarily on the land were less specialised and would not necessarily be sold with it.

Similarly, the lists of slaves who were manumitted (cf. the next chapter) are said not to show many explicitly listed as farming slaves, though in fact the numbers of farmers mentioned are not negligible: in documents from the years 330-320 BC 11 out of 85 manumitted slaves are 'farmers', two are specialist vine-dressers – 15% in all; there are five to eight leather-workers, six retailers, five merchants, and some retail-sellers. But many are given no occupation, and are either domestics, or all-purpose slaves who may well have done work on the farms. Further, craft-workers, especially those allowed to work on their own, would be more likely to be manumitted than farm-hands; so one would expect the latter to be under-represented on such lists.

The picture of peasant farmers and their households in the comedies of Aristophanes is often believed to provide the best evidence for the presences of a few slaves on the small farms of relatively poor peasant citizens. In these plays 'comic heroes' presented as poor but decent citizens frequently have a number of all-purpose slaves who may well do farming work. Since these are comedies, whose plots regularly mix fantasy and wild ideas with satirical treatment of contemporary individuals and themes, it is difficult to be sure how far to press a point like this. Perhaps the most convincing case is Aristophanes' last comedy, *Wealth*, where the hero Chremylos complains much of his poverty, and the whole play gives a strong impression of Athenian peasant-citizens suffering in the aftermath of the Peloponnesian War; yet Chremylos has his main slave, Carion, and a couple of other slaves as well (e.g., l. 26). One could argue, on the other hand, that this reflects a comic convention of the peasant-citizen, rather than contemporary reality.

Some general evidence which suggests that ownership of slaves was widespread among the citizens may conveniently be cited at this point. It seems in narratives of Athenian campaigns to be assumed that all hoplites went on campaigns with one slave attendant or 'batman' (e.g., Thucydides, 3.17, 7.75); and we might suppose that they would also have left one or more slaves behind to work on the farm or business under the supervision of another member of the family. Hence hoplites, it may be suggested, had at least more than one slave on average. More generally, several statements in law-court speeches seem to imply that all or nearly all Athenians were slaveowners. The most positive statement comes in a law-court speech which claims that slaves' evidence against their masters should not be trusted:

> In my view, it is right for you to think of this trial not only as a private matter of the litigants but as one of public concern to everyone in the city. It is not just these men who have slaves, but all the others have slaves too; and when the slaves look at what has happened to these slaves, they will cease to consider what good they can do for their masters in order that they may be set free, but rather will consider what false information they can lay against them.
>
> (Lysias, 5.5 = *GARS* 74)

Again, one speaker who admits he has no slave at the moment is a man claiming to be disabled and seriously poor, who is pleading that his disability pension should not be removed (Lysias, 24.7 = *GARS* 85). He claims that he would be in real trouble without the pension, and that 'I have as yet no children to provide for me. I have a craft which is little able to help me, which I can myself only work at with difficulty, and I cannot yet afford to buy someone to take it over.' The man was probably lying about his wealth, but he seems to be depending on the assumption that it was the sign of quite serious poverty for a craftsman to be unable to afford even one slave. It seems likely then that, realistically or not, the Athenian jury liked to be told that a great many ordinary Athenians owned slaves. This may be because in fact the jury itself tended to be composed of relatively well-off or even prosperous citizens, or that it wished to be spoken to as if it were so (this point too is the subject of much debate).

Even so, this line of argument suggests that if there was a very widespread assumption that all citizens, if at all possible, owned at least one or two slaves, this would affect the lives of peasants as much as craftsmen based in the city of Athens or the Peiraeus. The result would be that all citizens would buy slaves if they possibly could, as a mark of status and respectability, so as to appear proper members of a slave-owning democracy, even if the purchase of a slave was not certainly going to increase the profitability of their farm or business. If an Athenian could not find enough employment for his male slave (or slaves) throughout the year, he might be able to hire him (or them) out for other agricultural work or for carrying stone for the building trade. It is very likely, as has recently been argued by Gallant, *Risk and Survival* 30-3, that poor households may often have invested in a slave or two when times were better, or when the household had fewer actively working members, and sold them again when they found it unavoidable.

The cost of slaves is clearly important to this debate, but it is not a decisive factor. Slaves seem, comparatively at least, to have been relatively inexpensive (figures, limited as they are, suggest that prices ranged from c. 70 drachmai at the cheapest to several hundred, with unskilled slaves widely available at between 150 and 200). But it would still take a considerable capital outlay, or a sizeable loan, for a poor family to acquire a new slave, especially if it was not certain that the slave would be productively employed most days. The amount needed would, typically, be not much less than what a labourer on a public building might earn in a year, or twice the cost of an cow or ox, though cheaper than a mule.

The political implications of these views:
agricultural slavery and democracy
The political implications of the 'minimalist' view would be as follows: the connection between slavery and the development of the peasant-democracy is that the rich landowners, using slaves (or tenants, often ex-slaves or metics) for most of their agricultural labour, did not have to 'squeeze' the free peasantry for extra labour or rents in order to make

their surplus. But the operation of the democratic constitution and the inheritance laws kept the small-scale peasant holdings stable, and most of these peasants – the majority of the citizens – owned no slaves themselves. Hence, on this view, while the democracy would have been under much greater pressure had slaves not been available on the estates of the rich, enabling some of them to devote much of their time (and some of their wealth) on active political careers and on their leisure, the main supporters and beneficiaries of the democracy did not themselves directly exploit slaves, but operated their farms essentially with family labour, neighbourly co-operation, and short-term hired labour. On all but the first, extreme 'minimalist', views, Athens would still qualify as a 'slave-society', in that the major surplus for the élite came from slave labour; and the democracy depended on slavery since many of the rich allowed political and economic freedom to the peasants in part because they had their own slave-based wealth.

The political implications of 'maximalist' views would be to extend the direct dependence on slavery to many, or even to very many, of the citizens. On these views the dependence of rich landowners on agricultural slaves is increased (the use of tenancies and hired labour becomes minimised, and many of the tenant-farmers would themselves use slaves); but more than this, many of the ordinary peasant-citizens were somewhat richer, as well as more self-confident, independent and leisured, because they owned slaves. This would not be to say, of course, that they did not need to work themselves, with their slaves; but it would say that they did depend, even if only to a small extent, on the use of one or more slaves for part of their wealth, and found it easier to engage in some political activity as a result of their slaves keeping the work going in their absence.

Tentative conclusions

Decision between these views is not easy. My own choice would be tentatively to adopt, in general, a less extreme version of the 'maximalist' view, with the important qualification that the extent of slave-owning probably varied considerably over time. I would suppose that most if not all hoplite farming households had a few – all-purpose – slaves, much of the time, and a few of the better-off households of *thetes* had one or two, some of the time, even if such slaves were not fully employed on the land. Rather more strongly, I would hold that slave-holding was regarded as a most desirable feature of freedom and citizenship, which the Athenians, rightly or wrongly, liked to believe was very widely shared among them, though it is possible that the reality did not fully match this ideal, or, perhaps, did so more at some times than at others. Slave-holding, and the use of slaves in agriculture, were probably at their highest during the most prosperous years of the Periclean Age, before the Peloponnesian War.

Slavery in mining, building, manufacture and trade

In the other major sectors of the economy that developed rapidly in the fifth century BC, the evidence for slave involvement is much more satisfactory. First, the silver mines in the Laurion area of S. Attica produced considerable quantities of wealth both for Athens and for many individual Athenians, and were worked predominantly with slave labour. As excavations have revealed, mining in the region dates back to the sixteenth century BC, but the great expansion of operations began in the 480s BC, just in time to be used for the fleet that won the Persian Wars for Greece. For the rest of that century, until the disruptions of the Decelean War, the mines produced significant state-wealth and made many individual fortunes, for example, for politicians like Callias and Nicias. There was a slow recovery in the early fourth century, which gathered pace from the 360s onwards.

Our knowledge of the mechanics of the Laurion mines has been greatly advanced by excavations which reveal many mineshafts and tunnels (often running quite deep), and the associated washeries, cisterns, smelting ovens and slave-accommodation, over a wide area of the hilly country of southern Attica. For the legal procedures under which mines were opened up, leased, and made profitable, we depend on some literary references (such as Xenophon's pamphlet of the 350s, the *Revenues*, recommending an increase in the exploitation of the mines), and above all on fourth-century inscriptions recording the state officials' leasings of concessions. Some details are obscure, but it seems that the owner of the land on and under which the workings took place was normally responsible for the 'infrastructure' of shaft-works and so on, and received a regular rent from the lessees (where they did not lease the operation themselves). Lessees also made payments to the state (which owned the rights to the mines) for leases of periods of years (often three for mines in operation and seven for abandoned ones), and presumably then sold the silver thus mined for their profits to the state (which could coin it) or elsewhere.

Very occasionally we hear of free men engaged in manual work in the mines, but in general the unpleasant, dangerous and unhealthy

Fig. 4 A deep mine-shaft from Thorikos, a large coastal deme in the heart of Laurion silver-mines area in S. Attica.

Fig. 5 A photograph of one of the largest and best-planned surface workshops with ore-washeries from the Laurion area, Ergasterion C at Agrileza: such compounds also had cisterns either within them (as here) or nearby to store rain-water (constantly recycled in the washing process) and rooms for ore-crushing, milling and other activities, and for the personnel (slave and free) to eat and sleep.

Fig. 6 A reconstruction drawing of the ore-washing process, from the washery. A compound at Agrileza.

work was done by the most expendable slaves, and other, less dangerous, work on the surface by other slaves. Such slaves would be bought or hired by the lessees. Presumably new lessees could take over miners already at work on a site, and no doubt slaves who survived to be too old for underground work could continue to be used in the washeries or the smelting works.

Numbers of slaves working at different times cannot be recovered with any certainty. Xenophon records that Nicias (the unsuccessful general of the Sicilian expedition) at a time of high production in the fifth century owned 1,000 slaves whom he hired out for mining work under the control of a highly valued Thracian slave called Sosias. Sosias paid him an obol a day per man, and replaced casualties. Others owned several hundred mining slaves, others a lot fewer (*Revenues* 4.14 = *GARS* 87, and *Memoirs of Socrates* 2.5 = *GARS* 97). Such figures, and the archaeological evidence so far uncovered, makes estimates of 10,000+ slaves not unreasonable for times of high production. Silver-mining, then, a highly significant sector of Athens' economy, making major contributions to her military and economic successes, rested almost entirely on the most ruthless and cruel exploitation of large numbers of slaves. It clearly had a major impact on the landscape and the communities in the region: for example, we find a large number of heavy stone towers throughout the region, which suggests that those engaged in agriculture there felt the numbers of mining slaves a threat to their own security and that of their slaves and goods.

Slaves were also used extensively in the manufacturing of goods (such as weapons, pots, statues, knives, lamps, clothes). These were important sources of 'new wealth' during the fifth century for many families whose members then participated, often controversially, at the top level of politics. One need mention only the two late fifth-century so-called 'demagogues', Cleon, whose wealth was based on his family's tannery, and Cleophon, whose family owned lyre-making slaves. These were essentially cottage industries, where relatively few slaves worked in houses or small workshops. Many operated with just a few slaves. A typical example is the following, part of a list of properties allegedly inherited, and then dissipated, by Timarchos: 'nine or ten slaves, craftsmen in the shoemaker's art, each of whom brought him a daily income of 2 obols, and the leader of the workshop brought him three obols' (Aeschines, 1.97 = *GARS* 91). We hear of some larger establishments: much the biggest known is the orator Lysias' family, whose 120 slaves, most of whom manufactured shields, made them the 'richest of the metics' before their property was confiscated and some of them killed by the Thirty Tyrants in 404-403 BC (Lysias 12); next come Demosthenes' father's two workshops, with 32 or 33 knife-makers and 20 couch-makers, apparently bringing in annual incomes of 3,000 and 1,200 drachmai respectively (Demosthenes, 27.9 = *GARS* 86); and the ex-slave banker Pasion's shield workshop, allegedly worth 1 talent a year (Demosthenes, 36.11).

Public building – the great programmes on the Acropolis and elsewhere – used at times considerable labour, and a number of detailed inscriptions recording public payments to various workers enables us to see the modes of operations, and the involvement of citizens, metics and

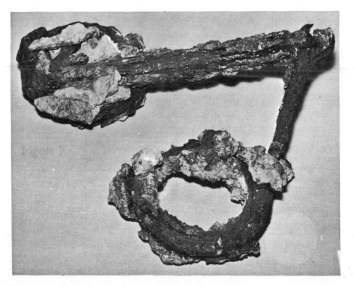

Fig. 7 Shackles, presumably for slave mine workers, found in the Laurion area: fourth-century BC.

Fig. 8 Manufacturing scene in a Foundry, making statues: clients can be distinguished from workers, and slave workers from freemen (slaves seem to be marked out by nakedness [apart from hats] and ugly features).

slaves. Quarrying (especially from the marble quarries on Mt Penteli-
kon) was presumably managed by individual payments to a smallish
number of contractors, who used slave-labour. The expensive business
of carting the stone was done by ox-teams and wagons, and this provided
occasional extra work for farmers and their slaves in slack periods of the
agriculture year. On the building site, the masons, sculptors and car-
penters to whom the state might give contracts are citizen or metic.
Metics outnumber citizens on our main source, the accounts of the
Erechtheion of the years 408/7-407/6, on which are found: 50% metics,
28% citizens and 22% slaves (there are useful extracts, with tables, from
this inscription in Austin/Vidal-Naquet, *Economic and Social History*
73.) These contracts were organised on a small scale: a contractor, with
or without a few slaves, would contract for individual pieces of work or
be paid by the day. Rates are 1 obol a day (on a comparable inscription
recording payments for an Eleusis building from the later fourth century
they have gone up to $1^{1}/_{2}$ obols). The status of the worker does not affect
the payment, whether day-rate or piece-work. All, whether described as
citizens, metics or as slaves belonging to a citizen or a metic, get paid
the same rates by the state-officials, though the master presumably was
– directly or ultimately – in control of the slaves' pay, whether he
received it and maintained the slave, or took his fixed amount and let the
slave live on his own on the rest. We have to envisage men of these varied
statuses working together on the columns and sculptures, masters along-
side their slaves in most cases. No one could then, or can now, distinguish
between the work of free man and slave.

In trade and banking, certain slaves were able to display skills of
book-keeping, agency and management, and rise to positions of considerable trust and responsibility. Perhaps the most important single reason
for this was that because of the widespread use of slavery free men were
reluctant to work directly for others, even in 'managerial' positions. The
most spectacular example concerns the banking family of Pasion, on
which more will be said in the next chapter.

While there was considerable variation in the living conditions of
these craftsmen and commercial slaves, a good many of them seem to
have had considerable day-to-day independence, and were described as
'those living apart' or 'wage-earning slaves'. In other words, such slaves
lived and worked on their own, in the workshop or shop, and were able
to keep some of their earnings to live on and to save towards later
manumission, while making regular payments to their masters. A good
example of such a slave in the area of overseas trade comes in a private
law-court speech of Demosthenes (34), where a certain Lampis, de-

scribed as Dion's 'slave' (*oiketes*) and as one along with others of Dion's 'boys' (*pais*) (34.5, 10) appears to be in control of a ship and to have engaged in what seem to be very shady dealings with various metics.

It is these slaves, able to work on their own and to travel about with money, often indistinguishable in dress and appearance from free men, whom right wing authors found extremely objectionable. Both the pamphlet written in the 420s known as the '*Old Oligarch*' and Plato speak sourly of the excessive freedom given to such slaves, and seem to resent the fact that one cannot hit them or treat them with contempt (Ps.-Xenophon, *Constitution of the Athenians* 1.10-2, Plato, *Republic* 563b). Doubtless, too, the more trusted and independent they were, the more likely they were to be permitted to form liasons with other slaves and breed, and equally to be set free and to be enabled to survive well as freedmen-metics.

Domestic slaves

This was perhaps the largest single category overall. As I have already emphasised, many all-purpose slaves would attend and serve their masters as well as doing productive work. Inside the house female slaves too had significant productive roles, as wool-workers, clothes-makers, bakers and so on. The manumission lists give 'wool-workers' as the commonest designation of slavewomen. Ischomachos' reports of his instructions to his young wife illustrate these points very fully, as he gives advice to her on how to organise the female slaves' work and control their behaviour with systems of rewards and punishments to encourage those that were hard-working and loyal. Two quotations give the tone of these instructions:

> I showed her also the women's area (*gynaikonitis*), divided by a bolted door from the men's area (*andronitis*), in order that nothing should be carried out from inside which should not be, and in order that the slaves (*oiketai*) should not breed without our approval. Good slaves are generally more loyal if they have children, but if bad ones cohabit together, they are more resourceful at devising mischief.

> After that we showed to the slaves (*oiketai*) who would use them where they should store the various utensils which they would need daily for baking, cooking, woolworking and so on, and handed the utensils over, telling them to keep them safely.
>
> (Xenophon, *Oikonomikos* 9)

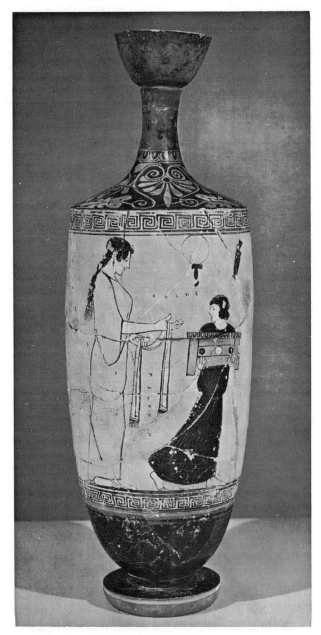

Fig. 9 A slave girl holding a box for her mistress, identified by cropped hair, and her duty.

In non-productive work in the richer households, considerable specialisation of slave-occupations is found. In literary sources and in inscriptions recording sales of slaves and manumissions we hear of butlers (literally 'table-managers'), housekeepers, maids, doorkeepers, *paidagogoi* (attendants for the male children), hairdressers and so on. A passage that has been taken (e.g., by Jones, *Athenian Democracy*) as implying that many of the better-off hoplites – those who paid the war-tax – did not possess a maid servant should in fact be read as suggesting that all did. Demosthenes' opponent is criticised for over-zealous collection of tax-arrears, breaking into the house pitilessly, and 'dragging bedclothes off the man and distraining on a maid-servant, if anyone was employing one' (24.197). The phrase seems to contain the amusing innuendo that the heartless tax-collectors enjoyed interrupting such a man when sexually engaged with the maid, and carrying off his favourite piece of property. On the other hand, even the rich seem not to have had huge slave-households on the Roman pattern; the numbers of domestics in such cases seems rarely to have exceeded 10 or 20. In less rich households, all-purpose slaves would have been the norm.

Prostitution and entertainment

Slaves and ex-slaves naturally were extensively employed in these areas. Prostitutes, male and female, were of widely varying levels of sophistication and price, from the expensive *hetairai* to the cheaper streetwalkers and brothel-dwellers; there were also flute girls and exotic dancers, butchers/chefs, and many other categories. All these slaves served the varied needs of the male citizens, from the luxurious upper class *symposia* to the cheaper pleasures available in brothels and bars. Athenians seem to have believed that their democratic state took care to keep such pleasures available to all their citizens at affordable prices (cf. Aristotle, *Constitution of the Athenians* 50, and Athenaeus, 569d-f): the fullest accounts of these activities and the values attached to them are to be found in Pseudo-Demosthenes' *Against Neaira* and Aeschines' *Against Timarchos*.

Public slaves

The state was also a large employer of slaves. No overall figures (or even guesses) are preserved, but they must have numbered several hundred at least, perhaps over a thousand. Most were menial employees attached to various boards of officials, doing work such as temple-repairs (inscriptions reveal an establishment of about 19 state-slaves working in the sanctuary at Eleusis, with some nine additional slaves used occasionally for stone-transporting, in the late 330s and early 320s BC), road-building, street-cleaning, work in the state-mint and the like (it was alleged, certainly falsely, that the father of the radical politician Hyperbolos had been a public slave in the mint: Andocides, fr. 5).

Other types of work, more surprisingly, could be done by state-slaves. What passed for a police authority in Athens, was a small board of citizen-officials, appointed by lot, called 'the Eleven'. They were provided with 'muscle' in the form of slaves to keep order in the assembly, the courts or other public places, to guard prisoners in the gaol and carry out executions, and occasionally to arrest criminals. Probably from the early fifth century to the early fourth century, a body of these slaves, specifically charged with keeping order in public meetings and public places, were known as the 'Scythian archers', forming a distinct corps, in theory of 300 men. In the sixth century 'Scythian archers' seem to have been a troop of mounted archers in the tyrant Peisistratos' army. But after the Persian Wars, perhaps deliberately in reaction against the tyrant's 'barbarian' allies, the new democracy bought a troop of slaves, some or all of them presumably from Scythia, to carry out the orders of the presiding magistrates. We meet these Scythians, an alien force in Athens, above all in Aristophanes' plays, where they are mocked for their coarseness, stupidity and poor command of the Greek language (see the funny scenes at the end of the *Women at the Thesmophoria*). The 'Scythian archers' drop out of our records early in the fourth century, and their functions were presumably taken over by fewer and less nationally identifiable public slaves, under the command of various magistrates.

Why did the Athenians use slaves, not citizens, to restrain, arrest and detain citizens? An important part of what being a citizen meant was not being manhandled by other citizens; and this natural sense of a citizen's honour and value was heightened by the fact that one did regularly beat slaves. This is well expressed, for example, in a revealing passage in Demosthenes' *Against Androtion* 22.49-58, the key sentence of which goes:

> If you (the jury) wished to look into what makes the difference between a slave and a free man, you would find that the greatest distinction was that in the case of slaves it is the body which takes responsibility for all their offences, whereas it is possible for free men, however great their misfortunes, to protect their bodies.
>
> (Demosthenes, 22.54)

If a citizen-official on state business arrested and physically restrained a citizen suspected of a serious crime, there was a risk of social tensions, of creating a personal hatred or feud that could lead to further trouble. Hence paradoxically if a slave, who had little or no personal status and could be regarded with contempt, performed this function, he could be seen more purely as an agent of the city. To be physically removed by the 'archers' would be indeed a humiliation (cf. e.g., Plato, *Protagoras* 319c), but there would be little risk of any pre-existing relationships – either of friendship or hostility, involving either corruption or pursuit of a feud – that could complicate matters; nor would the arrest in itself create such a feud.

Some other public slaves had jobs of much greater intellectual skill and responsibility: for example, the manager of the coins, weights and measures, keepers of the archives, clerks and other assistants to the council. Here again putting continuity of routine administration in the hands of slave-clerks avoided the risk of the state's record-keepers having their own political motives for the manipulation of records. This group were paid regular salaries, could accumulate some wealth, and were able to mix more freely in society than other slaves. One state slave, Pittalakos, in control of his own house and money, and operating a gaming business, pursued a homosexual relationship, it is alleged, with a very beautiful citizen-boy called Timarchos. He then got into fights and rows, had his gaming equipment broken, and was flogged mercilessly as if he were a humble slave; he tried to bring a legal action, but was forced to drop the case (Aeschines, *Against Timarchos* 54-65). This case suggests that some state-slaves had special status. Pittalakos was apparently free from the laws that said slaves could not 'love' free boys and were unable to bring legal actions themselves. On the other hand his peculiar status seems very vulnerable when he becomes embroiled in a vicious rivalry with powerful citizens; his enemies treated him brutally, like an unruly slave, and he lacked, understandably, the resources to carry through his lawsuit against ruthless and influential opponents.

Chapter 5
Slaves in Classical Athens:
Treatment and Hopes of Freedom

It is not easy to understand the relations between slaveowners and their slaves in classical Athens. They were certainly complex and varied, and we have to cope with the almost total lack of any evidence from slaves or ex-slaves themselves. In looking at the evidence we do have, whether we consider Athenian laws dealing with slavery, advice for the management of slaves, or casual references to slaves and their masters in a range of sources, it is important to remember that it is natural and normal for slaveowners to display contradictory attitudes to the nature of their slaves, and to the best way of dealing with them. Owners dealt with their slaves with a mixture of tension, fear and cruelty, on the one hand, and unease, self-deception, and occasional kindness, on the other.

Slaves and the law

We know much more about Athenian law than about the law of any other Greek state, though we do not know nearly as much as we would like about the details of the laws, and much less about the way the laws developed between Solon and the fourth century. We can say though that, as in many slave-societies, the laws were framed to serve at least three purposes, which were in part contradictory: first, to maintain and reinforce the fundamental distinction between slave and free people; second, to preserve the institution, above all by allowing masters a great deal of control over their slaves and deterring the slaves from committing 'offences'; and third, to offer the slaves some legal protection by setting some limits to the powers of masters over their slaves. The laws' provisions seem to work simultaneously with radically differing conceptions of the slaves. One set of conceptions seems to view slaves as property, as complete 'outsiders', permanently alienated from the community they lived in, or as something less than human beings; on the other hand, at times they are seen as beings with at least some elements of 'humanity'. Further, as will be seen below, in the area of commerce we can trace a significant change in the legal capacities of some slaves during the fourth century.

Slaves' inferiority in legal procedure

First, the access of slaves to legal processes was either non-existent or managed in a way which combined cruelty, irrationality, and the insistence on their status as inferiors. Slaves, like women, could not bring legal cases or be prosecuted in their own persons. Their masters were legally responsible for their slaves' actions, and would have to bring any case where a slave was wronged by another. These points form the basis of an argument in a law-court speech designed to prove that a certain Kerdon was in fact the slave of the speaker's opponent, Arethousios, and could therefore be claimed as part of his property by Apollodoros, the speaker, who was seeking to recover money which Arethousios owed to the state as a result of a previous conviction. Apollodoros (himself a son of Pasion the ex-slave, cf. below) claims that Arethousios had reared Kerdon from early boyhood, had received all the payments for the work Kerdon had done, and had 'obtained justice, and given it, whenever Kerdon had committed some offence, since he was his master' (Pseudo-Demosthenes, 53.19-20). A passage of Plato well brings out the implications for the life of the slave, and the horror with which it is regarded by the free man:

> ...that experience is not that of a man, being wronged, but it is the experience of some slave (*andropedon*), who would be better dead than alive, who cannot, when he is wronged and humiliated, come to his own defence or to the defence of anyone for whom he cares.
>
> (Plato, *Gorgias* 483b)

Torture

These rules show a firm belief that slaves, as inferior beings, should not have access to law as did free people (and above all as did male citizens: women, metics and other foreigners were also subject to various restrictions). This belief helped to produce the least acceptable of all the dubious features of the Athenian legal system: the evidence of slaves (which might often be of considerable importance in a case) could only be presented to a law court if it had been obtained while the slave was being subjected to a process of supervised torture. But the torture of potentially relevant witnesses was governed by complex procedures, and, remarkably, seems to have been used very rarely, if ever. In order that the evidence of a slave who might be an important witness to the facts of a case might be heard, one of the parties had to challenge the other either to offer up his slave for torture or accept the offer of his slave. But whoever owned the slave, the important point was that both parties had to agree that the slave should be tortured if his evidence was ever going to be heard. In the surviving law-court speeches we find a great many cases where speakers argue that the evidence of slaves under torture is a very sure way of discovering the truth, and the practice one of the best features of the legal system, since slaves did always tell the truth under this pressure (whereas other witnesses often lied); and in this case the relevant slave should have been subjected to it (e.g., Demosthenes, 30.35-7, Lysias, 4.12-17 = *GARS* 177). On the other hand we have many cases where litigants argue that slaves will only say what they think will please their master or the litigant they prefer or the one who is in charge of the torture process, and hence that they were right not to accept the challenge (e.g., Antiphon, 5.31-7, Demosthenes, 37.40-1).

This practice raises many problems. First the rule seems irrational, as those who resisted a challenge pointed out: slaves were not necessarily more likely to tell the truth under torture than when not subjected to such pressure. Alternatively, if judicial torture was supposed to be so effective, why was it not applied to Athenian witnesses? To understand how the Athenians accepted such a practice, we need to consider a number of related elements of their 'ideology'. First, the Athenians conceived 'giving evidence in court' in two quite different ways – not only, as we do, as one of the best means of discovering what actually happened, but also as a mechanism whereby prosecutors and defendants paraded in their support those who were prepared publicly to back their side. The status of witnesses, that is, contributed to their value to the litigant; but slaves had no status to speak of in such a context, and there may also have been a reluctance to allow masters to suffer as a result of their slaves' testimony given without their consent. More importantly, any open access to the courts was felt to be part of what it meant to be 'free', and had to be denied to the non-free. Furthermore, slaves, as inferior beings and usually non-Greeks, could not, it was thought, be relied on to tell the truth, even under oath, because they lacked a basic commitment to the values of the community and its religion. Another point is that free men who gave evidence ran the risk of subsequently being prosecuted for 'false witness', but slaves could not be sued – so perhaps they had to incur a more certain risk, of being tortured. Thus the conclusion made some ideological sense: if slaves had some relevant knowledge, they should surrender it, on the agreement of both parties, in a way that emphasised their inferiority and built on one of the basic distinctions between slave and free, that punishments and beatings could be imposed on the bodies of slaves, but not on those of the free. A law of uncertain date specifically excluded Athenian citizens from judicial torture. But this ideologically appropriate solution seems to have produced almost no actual evidence in the courts. We have 42 cases in our law-court speeches where a challenge to collect evidence from a slave under torture is made. In 40 of them the opponent rejected the challenge on one argument or another, and in the other two an apparent agreement to proceed broke down in practice and the slave did not give his evidence (Isocrates, 17.12-16, Demosthenes, 37.40-2). We cannot say that such torture *never* took place and litigants' assertions that it often did were totally fictitious; clearly the procedures for making challenges, appointing torturers and so on were well-understood. But it does appear to have been extremely rare. The rules were drawn up in such a way that one or other side was almost always going to find it in their interests to avoid going through with the procedure, above all because they feared that the slave's testimony would go against them. It is conceivable that in some cases masters might also not wish to see a favourite, or a valuable, slave subjected to pain or damage; but, of course, one could not admit to such a feeling in the courts since it would undermine the basic assumptions of the practice. Instead, litigants offer up for torture or refuse to release their own slaves (or, for example, a slave with whom one has been having an intense sexual relationship, Lysias, 4.13-17 = *GARS* 177), without any sign of regret or pity. Ironically, however, the need to keep a slave away from the torture may occasionally have led to some slaves being declared to be free (cf. e.g., Pseudo-Demosthenes, *Against Timotheos* 49.55).

The Athenians seem never to have recognised and changed the obvious deficiency of this system that, in place of hearing the evidence of slaves, juries had in most cases to consider what to deduce from the fact that one or other side had refused to let them be tortured. Instead, they allowed this bizarre situation to continue – such was the strength of the ideological pressures to keep access to the courts and the giving of evidence a privilege only open to the free, and to preserve the interests of the slaveowners.

If, however, serious state interests were being involved, investigating magistrates or the Council could insist on masters surrendering their slaves to be tortured to tell what they knew (e.g., Andocides, 1.64, investigations into the mutilation of the Hermai in 415). In such cases, where the state felt it was at risk, the masters' interests could be overridden and it is in such cases that we have evidence for torture being applied to slaves, and perhaps also to foreigners. In similarly serious political or religious cases, slaves could be rewarded for informing against their masters. If they volunteered to make denunciations they could do so before the assembly or the council, and might also be given immunity from punishment and probably also subsequent freedom if their information was found to be accurate (cf. Lysias, 5, 7.16-17); but they would be killed if they were found to have been lying.

Substantive law

Slaves were often treated legally as part of the property of their masters, able to be bought, sold, bequeathed or confiscated like land or beds. As persons, their private lives were dependant on their owners' wishes; they could not form sexual relationships without their masters' approval, and any partners or children they had might legally be sold to live elsewhere without their having the slightest say in the matter (and such family disruptions of course have regularly caused the greatest distress in slave-owning societies). As we saw in chapter 3, the distinction between slave and free was further reinforced by specific laws precluding slaves from exercising in wrestling-grounds or being the lovers of free-born boys. In sexual matters, the main idea seems to have been that slaves, like women, had to accept that their bodies might be penetrated by free males, but they might not themselves penetrate the bodies of the free, male or female; male comedy (e.g., Aristophanes, *Women at the Thesmophoria* 490-2) imagined married women allowing their male slaves to service them as among the most dreadful offences wives were apt to commit (we have no way of knowing how often it happened).

But if slaves committed any offences, their mental responsibility was naturally taken into account by the laws. If it was held that the master had given orders to the slave, he was sued directly, and paid any penalty; if the slave was held to be responsible, the legal action would name the slave, but the owner would have to bear the defence and pay any fines imposed. He would doubtless himself punish the slave as he felt appropriate, if the court did not impose a physical penalty on the slave, and it is probable that the penalty might in certain cases be the surrender of the slave to his opponent.

Protection for slaves

On the other hand, the laws did seek to offer some minimal protection to slaves against 'excessive' ill-treatment. First, the death of a slave was treated legally as the killing of an inferior person. If a slave were killed by some one other than his or her master, the master could bring a prosecution against the killer (and a slave's relatives, if any, might urge such an action); this is shown by Pseudo-Demosthenes, *Against Euergos and Mnesiboulos* 47.71-2. The Athenians held that homicide was a most serious crime, and that a religious 'pollution' could endanger those who protected or came in contact with a killer who had not paid the appropriate penalty. These feelings certainly meant that anyone who killed a slave under any circumstances would feel obliged to undergo a purification ceremony (Antiphon, 6.4), and they might well encourage a master to take legal action against his slave's killer, and perhaps to bring a charge of homicide rather than merely for 'damage' to his property. Such cases, significantly, were heard at the same homicide court which heard cases of unpremeditated (i.e. less serious) homicide against citizens, and all cases of homicide against metics and foreigners; we do hear of a couple of cases of slave-killings being brought (Isocrates, 18.52, Demosthenes, 59.9 – both allegedly trumped-up cases). Whether a master actually chose to bring such a case on behalf of a dead slave would clearly depend both on his relationship with the slave and with the alleged killer; but the will to prosecute was less strong and the penalties were less severe than if a citizen were killed.

If a master killed his own slave, in theory he was committing a crime; if he felt his slave deserved the punishment of death he was apparently supposed to persuade the city's authorities to sanction an execution (cf. Antiphon, *On the death of Herodes* 47-8 = *GARS* 181). But if a master killed his slave and then purified himself, it is hard to see circumstances in which anyone else would bring a legal action, unless the slave perhaps had been about to lay information against him, or an enemy of the master took the case up as part of a sustained legal attack on him.

Grossly insulting ill-treatment short of killing, by the master or another, was in theory covered by the law of *hybris* (discussed in ch. 3), which included slaves, women and children as possible victims. Here is how Demosthenes congratulates an Athenian jury on its humanity in this aspect of that important law:

> You hear, Athenians, the humanity of the law, which does not think it right that even slaves should be treated with *hybris*. Well then, by the gods, if one were to take this law to the barbarians from whom the slaves are imported to Greece, praising you and describing the city of Athens to them, saying 'there are some Greek people so gentle and humane in their manners that although they have often been wronged by you and naturally

UWE, BRISTOL LIBRARY SERVICES

have an ancestral hostility towards you, even so, the slaves whom they have acquired by paying a price for them they do not think it right to treat with *hybris*, but have publicly made this law to prevent it, and by now they have inflicted the death penalty on many who broke this law.'

(Demosthenes, *Against Meidias* 21.48-9 = GARS 183)

One cannot believe all of this rhetoric, of course, and certainly not that many Athenians were executed for *hybris* against slaves (no names are given). The idea that the Athenians offered more protection and freedom to their slaves than did other Greek states (above all perhaps Sparta with her helots) is found elsewhere (as we saw in ch. 4, the '*Old Oligarch*' and Plato disapproved of it); but it would not have been easy for anyone to know how true that was. The law assumes that slaves were not only 'persons' but had some minimal honour that deserved to be protected, and, as we saw, it was probably introduced in the sixth century when slaves were not so uniformly non-Greek; but it remained an important part of Athenian thinking about slaves in the classical period. It is very difficult to believe that in practice even extremely sadistic treatment of a slave by an owner would impel another citizen to bring a prosecution, except in wholly unusual circumstances. Where a free man maltreated another's slave, his or her owner might well be more likely to bring a less serious charge of 'damage' – which would bring financial rewards – than of *hybris* against the wrongdoer. In either case presenting evidence to the court would be a major problem, given the slave's lack of legal access. One could suggest, at most, that the law was felt to endorse a vague, and rather complacent, sense of some minimal moral obligation to see slaves as people with some status, which may possibly have had some slight practical effect on the behaviour of slaveowners. This was certainly of much less significance than the main effect of the law, extending to all male citizens the right not to be insulted, or treated 'like slaves', by richer fellow-citizens (cf. Demosthenes, *Against Meidias* 180-1). Demosthenes (*Against Meidias* 46), like Aeschines (*Against Timarchos* 15-17), emphasises also the importance of punishing all types of *hybris* in order to protect the citizens.

The only other legal recourse open to appallingly maltreated slaves was to run away and seek asylum in the shrine of the Furies or the temple of Theseus in Athens. There they could demand that they be sold to another master, and if one was prepared to buy them, the master was expected to sell. If this failed and the slaves had to return to their existing masters, the masters were supposed not to punish them (cf. *GARS* 222-3).

How often this procedure was operated, and with what results, is completely unknown.

Moral qualms among slaveowners are likely to have been felt more strongly towards those slaves who were especially trusted by their masters, working and living on their own as business managers or shipping agents and so on. It remains a little unclear how far the law developed to allow such slaves to form binding contracts with those with whom they did business. But it seems that at least from the middle of the fourth century onwards, in the specific category of 'commercial cases' where greater use was made of written contracts than in other areas of Athenian life, slaves operating fairly independently could appear in court as witnesses, prosecutors or defendants as if they were free. In these courts metics and foreigners too had equal status with citizens. The chief evidence for this is Demosthenes speech 34 (mentioned in ch. 4), which focuses on the trading and legal activities of the slave Lampis. In these ways the Athenians allowed some of the normally strict distinctions of status, with their contradictory effects, to be relaxed in the important area of commercial law.

Treatises on household management

There exist a few examples of general advice on how to treat slaves, in Xenophon's *Oikonomikos*, written c. 360 BC (see *GARS* 205), in Plato's *Laws* (*GARS* 80, pp. 83-4), and in another *Oikonomikos* written by one of Aristotle's pupils (*GARS* 206). Naturally, these tend to be somewhat optimistic, bland and idealised. Their main concern is for owners to achieve the slaves' docility, hard work and good will, to advise the right balance between firm control and inducements and incentives, and thus to make the institution work as well as possible. While they share many points and perceptions, there are some interesting differences; in all these works there seems at first sight to be some concern for the interests of the slaves themselves, but it is very debatable how far this goes.

These works are all reluctant to describe details of punishments, and Xenophon in particular, largely followed by Pseudo-Aristotle, places greater emphasis on rewards in slave-management, though Plato criticises over-use of the whip and goad, while emphasising the need to be 'firm'. But one should not miss the point that all recognise that such physical punishment is an essential element in management and that slaves pay with their bodies for their offences, while the free do not. Plato, indeed, in his detailed legal proposals, also imposes strict, often savage, penalties for offending slaves.

Xenophon's advice on incentives clearly operates with inconsistent conceptions of the nature of slaves, which in part is related to a distinction between those suitable as workers and those capable of acting as foremen in command over the other slaves. Thus at times he recommends treating them like wild animals, training them with punishments and rewards of extra rations, supported by differentiated clothing and shoes. But at other times he views slaves as human beings, who react like free men and women, recognising that some slaves 'love honour' and 'crave praise', and recommending that they be rewarded accordingly. Finally he claims (with much rhetorical exaggeration) that one may treat especially honest and loyal slaves 'as free men, not only making them rich, but also honouring them as if they were gentlemen' (*Oikonomikos* 13-14; cf. also 9.5 = *GARS* 193, quoted in ch. 4 above, where bearing children is a privilege only allowed to 'good' slaves).

Much the same picture is given by Pseudo-Aristotle, though in a rather more realistic tone. He recommends treating slaves according to their deserts, repressing the potentially disobedient without excessive cruelty, but rewarding good slaves with extra food, with honours, and with a share in the holidays provided by festivals. He adds, what Xenophon surprisingly omits (unless that is what is implied by the phrase quoted just above, which seems unlikely), that the prospect of freedom is a major inducement (cf. also below), and is both 'right and beneficial' (whether he means 'right' for the slaves' interests, or for the institution as a whole is unclear). He also suggests, however, that allowing them to have children is a useful means of retaining obedience, as the children act as 'hostages'. In a rather different way, Plato fears that many Athenians may be over-indulgent with their slaves, and that this allows a dangerous narrowing of the necessary gap in aptitudes and intelligence between slave and free. Yet he also insists that one should give the slaves appropriate honour 'not only for the slaves' sake, but for the good of the masters': masters should not treat slaves with *hybris* or injustice, because it makes the slaves' 'souls' more sullen and rebellious and the souls of the masters more depraved (*Laws* 777b-778a).

These debates can be easily paralleled, in their anxieties and contradictions, with the much fuller evidence of the southern United States. One can see these uncertainties equally in the pamphlets of slaveowners and in the narrative of the intelligent and articulate ex-slave Frederick Douglass. Douglass, for example, gives an account of how when he was treated most savagely he rebelled with violence and ingenuity to recover a sense of his own manhood. But he also asserts that it was on the rare occasions that slaves were treated with kindness and humanity that they conceived the greatest desire to attain full freedom – not just to have a good master, but to have no master.

Freedom for some slaves: manumission

The inducement of freedom was a strong weapon in the slaveowners' armoury. To use it, of course, one had to overlook the fact that to set a slave free as a reward for good behaviour conflicts with the idea that 'barbarians' (or 'blacks' in some other slave-societies) were naturally suited to living as slaves (cf. ch. 6). But it had so many advantages that this ideological problem did not in practice usually worry slaveowners. Such was evidently the case in ancient Greece.

One potential source of large-scale state manumission was as a result of military service, though its use was rare and restricted to the most desperate crises. It is important to emphasise that in the Greek city military service was a prime duty and privilege of the citizen. Metics (like *periokoi* at Sparta) might be held to have enough of a stake in the community to contribute in calculatedly subordinate roles to the Athenian army and navy. But slaves were not, and as a result were admitted into the army or navy only as a last resort in cases of emergency, and were often offered manumission and in some instances a form of citizenship in advance. This happened at Athens perhaps before Marathon in 490, and certainly in the last few years of the Peloponnesian War (cf. Aristophanes, *Frogs* 33-4, 290-1, 693-4). In other states, freeing of slaves for use in army or navy may perhaps have occurred a little more frequently (and cf. the Spartan use of helots discussed in ch. 3). The desperate needs of a civil war, in particular, might produce such appeals to slaves. This happened in Corcyra in 427 BC, where slaves in the countryside were offered freedom by both sides and the majority of them chose to help the democrats (Thucydides, 3.73).

Other cases of manumission were the gift of individual masters. The attraction of freedom to slaves, under any terms, is all too clear. Life as a slave meant having the consciousness of your inferiority, lack of rights and lack of social identity constantly brought home to you, as you were subject to your masters' commands, and to whatever beatings, sexual exploitations or other deprivations and humiliations might be inflicted or threatened. Hence many slaves, especially those working inside the household, or those working with relative independence, could, it seems, be persuaded fairly readily to work efficiently and loyally over periods of years by the prospect of eventual liberation.

In practice, selective manumission carried a great many advantages for masters. Many slaves would only be set free towards the end of their lives (and most would not in fact live that long) when perhaps their value as slaves would be declining. Rather than having to continue to feed, out of sentiment, a possibly diminishing and unsaleable asset, selling him or her for whatever one could get, or, finally, simply casting the slave out to beg, or to die, a master could seem generous by disposing of the faithful slave by a formal and legally recognised grant of freedom. Often, too, slaves would be set free towards the end of their master's life, or under the terms of his will. The attraction of such arrangements to owners, and the possible benefits of also manumitting selected younger slaves, become clear when some of the conditions commonly imposed are considered. First, slaves would regularly agree to 'buy' their freedom, using one or both of two mechanisms. They might give their master some of the money they may have been accumulating over the years, that is part of their wages or whatever he had permitted them to keep. Or they might scrape together a collective contribution (*eranos*), that is an interest-free loan from their friends, already freed relations, or lovers (for the case of the celebrated *hetaira*, Neaira, whose lovers contributed to her *eranos* see Pseudo-Demosthenes, *Against Neaira* 59.29-32). Thus these ex-slaves contributed their savings or their friends' contributions to help their former masters to buy new slaves as their replacements.

Second, manumitted slaves did not become completely free. In the Greek world they did not become citizens, as they did in Roman Italy. In Athens freedmen acquired metic status, and like metics had to register with an Athenian citizen as their patron and legal representative. This would be their former master; in cases where the master was himself a metic, his citizen patron would probably become the freedman's patron as well. As metics, freedmen had to pay the special metic-tax (12 drachmai a year for males, 6 for females); and as ex-slaves they were usually subject to other obligations (though our information for these matters in Athens is extremely sketchy). We hear of the 'laws of freedmen' at Athens, and that freedmen who failed to keep their obligations were liable to a charge of 'desertion' (*dike apostasiou*, cf. *GARS* 27). It is said by our source, the late lexicographer Harpocration, that acquittal on such a charge brought freedom from all remaining obligations for the ex-slave, but conviction brought re-enslavement. By analogy from evidence for other Greek cities, mostly in the Hellenistic period, a master could perhaps have imposed various extra conditions (in addition to the initial payment and his registration as patron), such as the duty to stay with and work part-time for his patron for a period of years, or until death (these are called *paramone*-agreements). The conditions of manumission were, hardly surprisingly, loaded very heavily in favour of the slaveowners, who exploited to the full the desperate desire of the slaves to be known as free. Furthermore, it is obviously only the slaves 'living apart', the traders, craftsmen and entertainers, who were likely to have been able to 'buy' their freedom while still young enough, and equipped with a skill, to make viable careers for themselves (and, like comparable freedmen in the towns in the slave-states of the USA, become themselves slaveowners).

It is very difficult to say how frequent manumission of slaves was in Athens; as usual there is no worthwhile statistical evidence. Xenophon, who, as we saw, seems not to mention manumission as an incentive, in another pamphlet written in the 350s regretted that there were currently a great many metics who were 'Lydians, Phrygians, Syrians and other barbarians of all types' (*Ways and Means* 2.3). This may reflect a consciousness that the proportion of ex-slaves among the metic population was sizable, perhaps that it was increasing. Aristotle, as well as Pseudo-Aristotle, strongly recommended manumission as an incentive for all slaves (*Politics* 1330a32-3), but it is not clear whether they were encouraging existing trends or making radical proposals.

Some fragmentary inscriptions (mentioned above p. 43; see *GARS* 27) survive which deal with manumission of slaves in Athens, but they present many problems. A series of inscriptions record the dedications of silver bowls worth 100 drachmai, each dedicated, it seems, as a result of an ex-slave's acquittal in a case of 'desertion'; major issues are uncertain because of gaps at crucial points in these texts. It seems likely, however, that they reflect a special procedure which was only in operation in the 330s and 320s BC. This appears to have established a system of formal registration of manumissions using a process of fictitious legal actions for 'desertion' which the freed slave automatically wins (thereby apparently gaining unconditional freedom); to which was added a requirement that the state should benefit by a registration fee in the form of the dedication of the bowl. What special conditions in Athens produced this procedure is unknown. It was perhaps part of the drive, master-minded by Lycurgos, then the dominant figure in Athens, to reorganise many areas of Athenian life, and to persuade Athenians to contribute financially, as in other ways, to the recovery of Athens after her defeat by Philip at Chaeronea in 338 BC. At about the same time, the practice was stopped whereby owners would gain publicity for their manumissions of their slaves by proclaiming them in the theatre at the festival of Dionysos (Aeschines, *Against Ctesiphon* 3.41, 44).

What proportion of manumissions used this peculiar registration procedure in this period, and what proportion used other methods, is unclear. But we have something like 300 dedications in this period of perhaps 20 years or less, on incomplete lists; and if this form of manumission was normally unconditional, and was more expensive, it may not in fact have been the most commonly used. The majority of occupations listed of the ex-slaves on these lists come, as would be expected, from those 'living apart'. Other sets of inscriptions from elsewhere in Greece, especially from Delphi in the Hellenistic period, suggest that unconditional manumission became less common than conditional from c. 200 BC onwards. The reasons are not clear, but may be related to a rise in the costs of replacement slaves as the market for imported slaves in Italy reached huge proportions.

In general, it seems to me plausible that the frequency of manumissions increased in Athens in the classical period and was related to the increase in slave involvement in trade and the crafts. In comparison with Rome the rate was certainly low, but it was perhaps considerably higher than in other slave systems, such as the plantation-economies in the USA or the Caribbean (though urban slaves, manumission, and slaveowning black freedmen were not negligible elements in the southern states). There are useful comparative tables and discussions, based, admittedly, on a mixture of good evidence and speculation, in Patterson, *Slavery and Social Death* ch. 10. Whatever the reasons for manumitting slaves, it is to be seen as a mechanism which served to strengthen, not to weaken, the institution of slavery as a whole, and was managed in ways which maximised the practical advantages to the slaveowners as well as increasing their reputation for decency and generosity.

Evidence for fear and for friendship

In assessing what our other literary sources can tell us of the treatment of slaves in Athens, two obvious points need stating at the start. The first is that there must have been very considerable variation in the quality, or misery, of the lives of different types of slaves. There can have been little to mitigate the horrors of the brief existence of work, punishments, inadequate rations, and diseases for those working, perhaps in chains, in the mines at Laurion. At the other extreme, the lives of faithful and trusted domestics, or craft workers or traders 'living alone', could include a sense of (partly) belonging to a family, interesting work, some pleasant sharing in festivals and other consolations of religion, and some prospect of eventual freedom. But one must never forget that even the most trusted of slaves, of whatever age, would still regularly be called 'boy' or 'child'. Not even the most privileged slaves were free from the prospect of physical punishment, or of violent or sexual abuse; none had any rights to their own time, for leisure or even sleep (cf. the telling joke about slaves' snoring in Aristophanes' *Clouds*, quoted below, p. 82). All faced the fear that at any moment, at the whim of the master, their hopes of freedom might be dashed, or a worse form of slavery imposed. This is nicely revealed in a law-court speech, where a husband, recounting how he investigated his wife's alleged adultery before killing the adulterer, tells the jury how he persuaded the slave-girl who went to the market and did other services, and was operating as go-between in the affair, to reveal what she knew:

> You can choose one of two courses, either to be whipped and thrown in the mill, and have a life of perpetual misery, or, if you tell me the truth, to get pardon from me for your wrongs, and suffer nothing.
>
> (Lysias, *Against Eratosthenes* 1.16-19)

The second point is that, once more, virtually all our evidence comes from the slaveowners, not the slaves, and in almost all cases from material publicly presented to a listening or reading audience of other slaveowners. While contrasting pictures or attitudes can be found, a certain amount of systematic idealisation of relations and glossing-over of intimate horrors is only to be expected.

Fairly frank awareness of the basis of the relationship in fear and terror can indeed be found (and ancient slaveowners, unlike those in the southern United States, were not constantly faced with pressure to justify the institution from those urging abolition in the northern states and elsewhere). A law-court speaker, making a point that he had offered his slaves for torture, claims he did so even though slaves might well delight in incriminating their masters 'to whom they are naturally most ill-disposed' (Lysias, *On the Olive Stump* 7.34-5). In a notable passage Plato recognised that slaves inevitably tended to hate their masters, longed for freedom, and would revolt collectively unless masters maintained constant vigilance. As he put it, graphically:

> 'If one of the gods were to take a man who owned fifty or more slaves and were to transport him and his wife and children to a deserted place, along with the rest of his property and his slaves, where no free man was likely to come to his aid, what and how great would be his fear, do you think, that he, his children and his wife would all be killed by their slaves?'

'His fear would be as great as possible.'
'Would he not be compelled to fawn on some of these very slaves, make them many promises, and set them free, though he had no wish to do so, and so be seen himself to be the flatterer of his own slaves?'

(Plato, *Republic* 578d-9b)

This passage shows the awareness of the slaveowners that it is only the uniform solidarity of all the owners in the community acting together as 'unpaid bodyguards' (in Xenophon's phrase, in a similar passage, *Hiero* 4.3), which kept the system going, backed by laws, ideological training, and in the last resort the whip and the possession of arms. Aristotle pointed out that one reason why citizens had all to undergo military training was to enable them to 'exercise the master's rule over those who deserve to be slaves' (*Politics* 1333b37-34a1). Furthermore, Athenians were also well aware that in order to avoid the far more serious dangers of revolt such as those faced by the Spartans from their helots, it was desirable to keep the slave-body, both in the community and in a household, composed of deracinated, unsettled and ethnically varied members who would have no obvious unity or common political purpose, nor any obvious haven if they ran away (e.g., Plato, *Laws* 777c-d, Aristotle, *Politics* 1330a25-8).

On the other hand there is considerable evidence of reasonably friendly and harmonious relations between domestic slaves such as nurses, boys' attendants (*paidagogoi*), or all-purpose slaves and the families they worked for. One passage from a law-court speech shows well how Athenians could seek to excite pity for loyal slaves and ex-slaves, and present themselves as considerate and kind. It illustrates other themes as well, such as the sizeable slave-holdings of richer Athenians, and the vulnerability of elderly female ex-slaves. The speaker is prosecuting his enemies, who at one stage of a protracted quarrel seized some sheep, a slave-shepherd and shepherd-boy, and then raided his farm-house just outside the city looking for goods in settlement of a court judgement; having failed to seize some slaves, they burst in on the house to seize furniture and valuables, and discovered the speaker's wife and children at a meal:

With her was an elderly woman who had been my nurse. This loyal and trustworthy woman had been set free by my father, and had then lived with her husband; after his death, since she was old and had no one to look after her, she came back to me.

I could not leave my old nurse in want, any more than I could
the slave who attended me as a boy. I was about to sail off as
commander of a trireme, and my wife wished me to leave such
a woman in the house with her.

(Pseudo-Demosthenes, *Against Euergos and
Mnesiboulos* 47.52-73)

Though the men were told that the money due was available for them at
a bank, they continued to seize what they could (while the rest of the
female slaves locked themselves in the secure 'tower' that was part of
the farm-building); but this old freedwoman, bravely clinging on to a
drinking cup, was so badly beaten as the men tore it from her that she
died five days later. The speaker decided, after taking advice, that
because the woman was neither his relative nor (any more) his slave, the
law did not permit him to bring a prosecution, and encouraged him to
seek revenge in some other way, which he was now doing in a string of
further legal cases.

We should recognise the plausibility of such individual cases and
the genuinely friendly emotions described, but we must also bear in mind
the self-interested motives of masters in treating certain slaves well, and
the probability that slaves and ex-slaves naturally had an interest in
feigning loyalty and friendship to make the best of their lives and to win
and preserve their freedom. In the nature of our evidence, we can have
no certainty about individual relationships revealed, let alone generalise
safely from them to the nature of relations in general between citizen
parents and the wet-nurses and attendants to whom they entrusted their
young children. Nor is it easy to assess the effects of such child-rearing
techniques; but their essential ambiguity is clear. As free children grew
up, they would be increasingly aware that they were expected to like,
and to obey in day-to-day matters of discipline, people whom they were
also expected to despise as wholly inferior and saw treated permanently
like children (e.g., in being regularly beaten), and often as casual sex-
objects. Many parents transferred major aspects of their childrens'
upbringing to slaves; this may have had some lessening effects on the
emotional bonding both between individual parents and their children
and between husband and wife. But we have to be very careful here;
despite the beatings, and the partial distancing, it would be rash to assume
too easily that close emotional relationships were not formed, or that the
pain of an infant's or child's death was significantly diminished; the
assumptions of the very small nuclear family of modern western
societies may be misleading when applied to the past.

Fig. 10 In this scene from a gymnasium (on a vase of c. 500 BC by Euphonius), the slave-attendant is identified both by his typically slave name – Tranion – and his job tending to the athlete's foot, rather than by his appearance, which is as idealised as the athlete's.

The evidence of Athenian drama has difficulties of its own. Slavery is, of course, assumed as natural and pervasive, but both the tragedies and the comedies raise questions about the ambiguities of the institution. In tragedies there are many faithful slaves such as nurses or *paidagogoi* in supporting roles. At times their apparent loyalty and goodness explicitly raises questions about the correctness of the assumptions of natural slavery that other characters in the plays often proclaim. Similarly, above all in some of Euripides' plays, themes of the horrors

of war and its aftermath, especially the sack of Troy, question the justice
of enslaving those defeated in war, especially the women and children,
and also the assumption of Greek moral and intellectual superiority (see
also ch. 7 below).

Comedies, both the fifth-century plays of Aristophanes ('Old
Comedy') and the fourth/third-century plays of Menander ('New
Comedy'), often focus on family activities and conflicts, and give
substantial roles to domestic slaves. On the one hand the exploitation
inherent in slavery is frankly recognised, and played for laughs. There
are constant references to physical beatings as the defining features of
slaves' lives, and not infrequently scenes of physical punishment on
stage are milked. There are constant jokes too about the comic citizen's
casual sexual use of slaves (and some jokes which suggest that the main
sexual activity male slaves can themselves engage in is masturbation).
Aristophanes was fond of claiming that he had given up a number of
stock comic routines, and in one such sequence he asserts:

> …and he dismissed the slaves,
> those running away, cheating their masters, and being beaten
>   on purpose,
> whom they drove out crying from the house, just so that
> a fellow-slave would laugh at his stripes and then ask him
> 'You poor thing, what's happened to your skin? Has a spiky
>   whip
> invaded your ribs in full force and laid waste your back?'
>   (Aristophanes, *Peace* 742-7)

But in practice he often resorted to such crude, even sadistic, stock
humour: for example, in an extended scene of slave-torture to discover
which, of the god Dionysos or his slave Xanthias, is the slave and which
the god (*Frogs* 605-73). Since the god is presented as a coward, the test
is inconclusive. Again, a few lines by the elderly peasant-rogue Philo-
cleon in the *Wasps* nicely bring out the ambiguity of relations: outraged
when his own slaves obey his son's orders to restrain him (subject to
punishment of chains and no food), he appeals to the Athenian hero
Kekrops:

> Will you look on and see me thus worsened by barbarian men
> whom I've taught how to bawl, four to the quart?

and to one of the slaves themselves:

> Won't you let me go now, you worst of beasts,
> don't you remember the time when I found you stealing grapes
> and I tied you up to the olive tree and flayed you well and
>   manfully,
> so that every one envied you? But I see you weren't grateful.
>
> (Aristophanes, *Wasps* 438-51)

On the other hand one development towards the end of Aristophanes' career, which is carried on with great force in the New Comedy, and in its Roman imitations, the plays of Plautus and Terence, raises a different and tricky question: how 'realistic' are the substantial and confident roles that can be given to slaves? Xanthias in the *Frogs* is a bold and cheeky slave, whose confidence contrasts with the weakness of his master Dionysos; Carion, on the other hand, Chremylos' greatly trusted slave in the *Ploutos* (Wealth), shares amicably and fully in his master's adventures, speaks boldly and rudely to his master's friends and wife, and argues vigorously with the wicked crook, the 'Sycophant'. In the New Comedy, among the different types of slaves encountered, the most striking character is the clever slave, who is not only often contrasted with his foolish young master but may also be the chief manipulator and problem-solver in the play, and has a 'love-interest' of his own. This pattern has been imitated and developed in innumerable later comedies in Western literature (for example, *The Marriage of Figaro* or Wodehouse's 'Jeeves' stories). Some scholars believe that this element in New Comedy provides evidence of an actual social development through the fourth century BC towards closer, more familiar and open relations between masters/mistresses and their favourite slaves; but it is probably rather to be seen as a useful comic convention, accepted by audiences, which bore no relationship to any general change in Athenian society.

Finally, one may mention one popular genre of literature to which slaves and ex-slaves may possibly have contributed, and which at times seems to reflect the feelings of slaves and other downtrodden members of Greek society – the fable. Fables, very often animal fables, were told throughout Greece, and used rhetorically to point morals or give political messages. From the fifth century BC on collections of fables were associated above all with one Aesop, supposed to have been a Thracian slave in the sixth century, who lived and was set free in Samos and became famous for his stories. But it is impossible to know which of the hundreds of fables later collected as Aesopian were actually told by him. Many of them can be seen to have some relevance to the lives of slaves:

for example, praising freedom with poverty over a cushy existence as a slave, encouraging the acceptance of existing hard labour for fear of suffering worse (e.g., by running away or changing masters), or (like the Brer Rabbit stories of the American South) celebrating the low cunning of the weaker animals.

A case-study: Pasion, Apollodoros and Phormion

The most famous and successful slaves we know about in classical Athens are the father and son Pasion and Apollodoros; their careers are totally exceptional, but full of interest. They reveal the maximum degree of social mobility possible in Athenian society. Pasion started working as a slave, probably in the late fifth century, in a bank owned by two partners who first gave Pasion his freedom, as he showed himself exceptionally proficient, and then left him in control of the bank. The first point then is that banking (that is, briefly, money-changing, money-holding, and some money-lending), above all urban activities in Athens, involved such professional expertise and trustworthiness that ex-slave managers were quite often left the business by the former owners, in preference to their own sons. Once a freedman-metic and in control of the bank, Pasion prospered, developed shield-manufacturing (thereby employing increasing numbers of slaves) and became rich enough to progress, in stages, to be granted full citizenship by decree of the Athenian people in recognition of his very generous grants of money and shields to the state. Once a citizen, he was now able further to diversify his interests into land, while maintaining the bank and the shield-making (metics were unable to own land). As a citizen, he could now also loan money to others on the security of their land.

   At his death his son Apollodoros, who wanted above all to be accepted as a rich citizen, and even as a gentleman and politician, found that the banking pattern was being repeated and the bank and other properties were not left directly to him but were leased to Phormion, an ex-slave freed by Pasion, with experience at managing the bank. Phormion was to act as guardian for the various properties until Pasion's younger son came of age; he was also to marry Pasion's widow Archippe, whose status was apparently left undefined when her husband became a citizen. Apollodoros unhappy with Phormion's management, contested the will in the courts, became involved in many other law suits over a period of years, and also began to play a part in Athenian politics. We know a fair amount about Apollodoros because a large number of law-court speeches delivered by him, or involving him, or the financial affairs of the bank, have been preserved, mostly among the speeches supposedly by Demosthenes. From his speeches, it is clear that throughout his financial and political career he was acutely, perhaps neurotically, sensitive about his origins as the son of a slave, and he exhibited also the disturbing snobbery and cruelty of the social climber, above all in his distasteful attacks on Phormion as an ex-slave and on his own mother for marrying him (Pseudo-Demosthenes, *Against Stephanos* 45). In fact, Phormion too repeated the pattern of success, became a citizen, and ran his own bank.

It is clear too that Apollodoros had to meet a lot of hostility and prejudice because of his origins, as he tried to win popularity by lavish expenditure on public services (like running a trireme), and to build a political career. He himself reports how on one occasion a rival trierarch justified causing him trouble by delaying taking over the running of the ship from him, as he was supposed to do, by saying to others 'the mouse has tasted pitch – he wanted to be an Athenian': that is, Apollodoros deserved to suffer a bit for being such an upstart (Pseudo-Demosthenes, *Against Polycles* 50.26). To move so fast from slavery to prominent citizenship was quite remarkable in Athens; and whereas freedmen might quite often be able to merge, over a generation, into the ranks of the metics, it was much more difficult for the son of an ex-slave who was a citizen to forget, or to be allowed to forget, his slave origins.

Chapter 6
Resistance, Flight and Revolt

Most chattel slaves in classical Greece, with little realistic hope of manumission, will have had good grounds for hating their masters and seeking a change or at least some retaliation. Domestic or independent slaves, encouraged to hope for freedom, might, one may suppose, react against delay or disappointment. This chapter briefly considers what means of resistance were open to chattel slaves, and why large-scale revolts were not more frequent, in contrast to the situation with the helots in Sparta.

Sabotage

Studies of slavery in the southern states have demonstrated a vast amount of all types of sabotage by disgruntled slaves, from malingering, tool-breaking, theft, slow-working, and brutality to farm-animals, to more serious acts of arson, self-mutilation, violence against masters or over-seers, and flight. In all, this seriously reduced the productivity of the system. The evidence from classical Athens, much less full as it is, presents comparable features; the economic effects naturally cannot begin to be quantified.

Advice to slaveowners emphasise the need for strict regimen and punishments to eradicate such defects. Xenophon provides a convenient short list (his Socrates is arguing against an advocate of a life of easy-going pursuit of pleasure):

> 'But let us consider how masters treat slaves of that type. Surely they bring their lustfulness under control through starvation; they prevent them from stealing by locking up the places from which they could take anything; they stop them running away by chaining them; they drive out their laziness by blows. Or what do you do, when you discover that one of your slaves is like that?'
> 'I punish them with every sort of hardship until I compel them to behave as slaves.'
>
> (Xenophon, *Memorabilia* 2.1.16)

Theft, often of food and drink, appears most frequently as the typical slave-crime. Xenophon (*Oikonomikos* 14.2) recognises that substantial stealing of crops by the overseer will affect profits. Isocrates, in an argument against the Spartan system of upbringing which praised effective 'stealing' of food by young Spartiates, claims that 'the rest of mankind regards as the worst of slaves those who commit crimes and steal', while the Spartans honour their young men who behave like that (*Panathenaikos* 12.214). It is also clear that if slaves were caught stealing outside their own households, the property-owners could beat or rape them without fear of prosecution from the slaves' owners (Pseudo-Demosthenes, *Against Nicostratos* 53.16, Aristophanes, *Acharnians* 271-5).

Aristophanes often makes ambivalent jokes about slave wickedness. In *Wealth* Chremylos 'praises' Carion in this double-edged way:

> Well, I will tell you; for of my slaves
> I hold you to be the most loyal,...and the biggest thief.
>
> (26-7)

And Carion, the Aristophanic slave with the closest relationship to his master, confesses such thefts – and subsequent beatings – later in the play in conversation with the gods' 'slave' Hermes (1139-45). The *Knights* begins with a scene in which two slaves (who are also Athenian politicians, since their 'master' is Demos, the elderly personification of the democracy) first consider running away or seeking asylum at a temple, and then steal some wine in order to aid their planning (1-110). In the *Frogs* Xanthias and a slave in the Underworld run through the minor instances of rebelliousness in which they delight, and which gives them some self-esteem – standing up to their masters, cursing them behind their backs, muttering abuse when leaving after a beating, interfering in their affairs, eavesdropping and passing on gossip to those outside the family (738-56). These types of jokes no doubt reflected the constant fears and anxieties of the slaveowners; yet in their comic contexts, and combined with the general picture of close and free-speaking relations between the average Athenian and his few slaves (which became increasingly unrealistic, as was suggested above), their total effect was perhaps more reassuring than alarming.

Flight

The threat of runaways was taken very seriously, and the more so the more valuable the slave (though flight in itself doubtless diminished the slave's value, to the master and to others). The general solidarity of slaveowners created a climate favourable to the recapture and return of runaways. So Xenophon displays a master's concern for the value of his slaves (as well as the greater importance of friends) by the following Socratic discussion:

> 'Tell me, Diodoros, if one of your slaves runs away, do you take care to recover him?'
> 'Yes, by Zeus,' he said 'and I summon others to help by proclaiming a reward.'
> 'And if one of your slaves is ill, do you care for him and call in doctors to prevent his dying?'
> 'Indeed I do.'
> 'Well, if one of your acquaintances, who is much more useful than your slaves, is in danger of being ruined by poverty, do you not think it worth while your taking care to save him?'
> (Xenophon, *Memorabilia* 2.10.1-2 = *GARS* 200)

As well as public rewards (and asking all one's friends and acquaintances to keep a look-out), owners apparently might employ some one to search out the runaway (a fourth-century comedy by Antiphanes was titled 'The Runaway-Catcher'). Slaves thus recaptured might find themselves permanently branded or tattooed, in addition to any other punishments. Aristophanes' chorus of Birds, inviting a collection of dubious characters to seek a better life among the birds, includes a 'branded runaway' who will be easily passed off as a speckled francolin (*Birds* 760-1).

Added to these disincentives, there was of course no country or place to which slaves could flee where they could be sure of protection, no abolitionalist havens such as the northern states came to provide for those enslaved in the Old South. Even so, small groups of bandits or outlaws operating in the mountains or the forests, or pirates raiding from the sea (not restricted to ex-slaves), might have provided new – albeit dangerous – shelters and careers for individuals or small bands of runaway slaves. Also, it may not have been impossible for a resourceful slave, prepared to claim to be a freedman or a metic, to survive undetected, at least for a time, in a fairly cosmopolitan urban environment of citizens, metics, freedmen and foreign traders, such as in Athens and the port of Piraeus. This would be more feasible if the runaways managed to acquire friends (or partners in shady dealings), or get away to another city. A short law-court speech by Lysias (23) is devoted to the disputed status of a character called Pancleon who had claimed, when faced with prosecution as a metic, to be a 'Plataean', that is one of the refugees from the small city of Plataea destroyed by the Spartans in 427 BC who were given Athenian citizenship, until their city was restored in 386; but the prosecutor claims that he is in fact a runaway slave. However, more than one 'owner' has been seeking to recover him. In the world of the divided city-states, each of which maintained extremely limited civic authorities and policing bodies, survival for runaways may have been easier than in the more bureaucratic regimes such as Hellenistic kingdoms or the Roman Empire; and yet catching runaways was certainly a problem in those societies too.

Chances of running away successfully were greatly increased in times of crisis, especially war and civil war. The Peloponnesian War provides a number of instances. The hoplites' slave-attendants might desert a losing army, as they did in very large numbers in the latter stages of the doomed Athenian expedition in Sicily in 413 (Thucydides, 7.75). In the early years of that war when the Spartans regularly invaded Attica, they, along with Athens' hostile neighbours Megara and Boeotia, were likely to have encouraged runaways. Hence Athenian masters were aware that unhappy slaves were more likely to think of running away in order to seek freedom or better conditions among the enemy, if Aristophanes' grumbling farmer Strepsiades in the *Clouds* is to be taken as reflecting real fears:

> The slaves are snoring; they wouldn't have before.
> Curse you, War, for many reasons,
> now that it isn't even possible to punish the slaves.
>
> (5-7)

Slightly harder evidence is provided by Thucydides' statement (discussed above pp. 42f.) that during the period 412-404 more than 20,000 slaves fled from the Attic countryside to the Spartans based at Decelea. If the Spartans had promised freedom to these runaways, they seem to have been disappointed; according to another good source the slaves were sold cheap to the Thebans (*Hellenica Oxyrhynchia* 17.3). Conversely, when in 411 the Athenians were ravaging the land of their ally Chios which was in revolt against them, Thucydides records:

> The slaves in Chios were many, and in fact were the most in any single city except Sparta, and at the same time, because of their number, they were punished more severely for their offences. So when the Athenian army seemed securely estab-

lished in their fortifications, the majority of the slaves immediately deserted to them, and, since they knew the land, it was they that did the most damage.

(8.40)

Whether these slaves were given any reward is not known. We do know, however, of a number of instances in the Hellenistic period where provisions to return runaway slaves were included in the treaties that concluded wars; see for example two documents in M.M. Austin's *The Hellenistic World from Alexander to the Roman Conquest* (Cambridge, 1981: nos 33 and 70). But it is important to observe that Thucydides, at least, clearly thought that many slaves would flee, swiftly, with enthusiasm and in large numbers, to the chief enemies of their masters when they saw what they presumably thought was some chance of improvement; and he also thought that savage treatment increased such readiness to try to escape.

Revolts

Large-scale cohesive revolts, as distinct from individual or mass flights, were extremely rare in Greek chattel slavery. The only substantial and partially successful movement of slaves in revolt of which we have a record occurred (once more) on Chios. Athenaeus followed his assertion that the Chians 'invented' chattel slavery with the pious statement that divine anger afflicted the Chians later. He then quotes a long account taken from the historical work of one Nymphodoros of Syracuse (writing probably in the latter part of the third century BC), the gist of which is as follows (Athen., 265c-266f = *GARS* 80, pp. 84-6). Slaves in Chios had for some time been running away in large numbers, forming bases in the forested hills and attacking their masters' country-houses. Under a new leader, the brave and resourceful Drimakos, the slaves successfully resisted a number of armed attempts to force them to give in. Drimakos, claiming the authority of an oracle, persuaded the Chians to accept a treaty providing peace and co-existence: he guaranteed to steal no more than fixed and agreed measures of loot, and to accept as new members of his community only those runaways who could demonstrate they had suffered intolerable treatment, sending the rest back. The deal worked until Drimakos grew old: both looting and runaways were kept to tolerable levels, and Drimakos imposed strict discipline on his people. But finally Drimakos (perhaps feeling the group might collapse on his death?) arranged for his 'boyfriend' to kill him, and claim the large reward for his head which the Chians had maintained (even though they had made the deal). Subsequently, however, uncontrolled ravaging by bands of runaways caused the Chian landowners to regret the end of Drimakos' regime, and they gave him a hero's shrine and offered him cult as the 'Kindly Hero'. Both runaway slaves, and masters whom he warned in dreams of slave-plots, made offerings to him.

These events are not precisely dated; they clearly took place some decades at least before the date of Nymphodoros, and so probably during the early third century, or somewhat earlier. One reason in particular for accepting the essential reliability of the account is that in Jamaica from the late seventeenth century onwards very comparable events took place. Groups of rebel plantation slaves (the 'maroons') established independent settlements in remote areas, which led after extended resistance and battles to very similar sorts of detailed treaties between the white authorities and some of the rebel bands (initially the one led by a certain Captain Cudjoe). Factors whose combination seem to help to explain such long-lasting revolts and eventual accommodations are: terrain suitable for guerrilla bands; relatively large numbers of slaves engaged on large estates and overall a high ratio of slave to free; the subjection of the slaves to especially savage treatment; and charismatic leadership that often makes effective use of religious claims. Whether in Chios, as in Jamaica, the prevalence of runaways followed some military or political troubles cannot be determined, given the uncertainty of the date. It must equally be emphasised that in Chios these fairly successful revolts led to an agreement with the slaveowners, in part because of the 'moderation' of the rebels, or perhaps because of their 'selling-out'; they agreed to limit their looting activities, and to maintain a level of public order and the institution of slavery itself, by returning slaves who had no case for running away. Whether other such cases have fallen from our records cannot be known.

This revolt, like the ones in Jamaica, though lasting for some time, probably did not involve enough numbers – of revolted slaves or opposing forces – to be considered as a full-scale war. In fact slave-revolts serious enough to be called 'slave-wars', engaging large armies on both sides, have been extremely rare in human history. One can name the major revolts in Sicily in 133-129 and 104-100 BC, Spartacus' war in Italy in 73-1 BC, and the revolt led by Toussaint l'Ouverture in Haiti at the time of the French Revolution. Many of the features probably found on Chios were also present in these rebellions, in greater numbers and to a greater extent, and they led to revolts where the leaders accepted all runaway slaves and managed to inflict very extensive damage on their former owners. Huge Roman armies were needed to suppress those in Sicily and Italy.

Conclusions

What conclusions should be drawn from the level of dissidence and revolt that can be supposed to have taken place in classical Greece? It is too glib, and reflects an excessively idealised view of Greek 'humanity', to conclude that there were few revolts because chattel slaves were given generally mild treatment. We have seen enough evidence of systematically cruel handling, physical abuse and judicial torture, and of theft, sabotage and flight, to doubt such a judgement. Other factors which help to explain why chattel slaves revolted collectively less often than the helots in Sparta are the severe personal disruptions of the uprooting from one's homeland and the sale to an owner, and the lack of common identity and cohesion between the slaves in any household or community, since they belonged to many different nations, languages and cultures; the relative absence of large slave-units in Athens, and probably most other states (if it is right to see Chios as something of an exception in this respect); and the vigilance and solidarity of the slaveowners and their laws. On the other hand some (relatively) less oppressive aspects of Greek slavery may have their part to play. Many slaves' accommodation to their terrible lot may have been helped by a partial incorporation into the life of a family, reinforced by some sharing in the ceremonies and enjoyments offered by the domestic and community sacrifices and festivals. Further, a good few slaves, including the more able and so the potential leaders of resistance, were probably persuaded to conform to their masters' wishes by being given extra privileges, more interesting jobs with some independence or power over other slaves, and some prospects of manumission. Hence many slaves in Greece adjusted to their condition either by accepting the values of their masters, or by using the appearance of such acceptance to make the best of their limited prospects, or by adopting, or seeming to adopt, an apparently simple, 'childlike' set of responses, lazy, docile, grinning and deceitful: what was called in the Old South the 'Sambo' type, and what Greeks referred to when they claimed that slavery takes away half a person's goodness or intelligence. As ever, it is finally the ambiguities of slavery, and the variations and uncertainties of treatment, prospects and responses, that stand out.

Chapter 7

Justifications: Barbarians and Natural Slaves

Slavery, in one form or another, was universal in the ancient cultures known to the Greeks; they grew up with it and accepted it, together with its inherent cruelty and contradictions, largely without question. Slight hints, however, of some intellectual unease are to be found from the late fifth century on, as part of the ferment of radical questioning brought to the Greek cities by the Sophists. Their theorising, and their debates with Socrates and his varied pupils, seemed to raise some doubts about the standard view that slavery was natural and just. But the dominance of this view was not seriously affected, particularly if the slaves were not Greek.

Slavery and the Greek/barbarian distinction

Originally, enslavement may been been accepted as a stroke of ill fortune which might happen to anyone, and which would then have a catastrophic effect on one's personality as well as on one's way of life. The view that foreigners ('barbarians') deserved to be enslaved, whereas Greeks deserved to rule, may have begun to spread during the sixth century as increasingly slaves were being imported from the neighbouring non-Greek areas. But it was undoubtedly the Greek victories in the great Persian Wars (490-480 BC), and the subsequent extension of Athenian sea-power to areas previously ruled by Persia throughout the Aegean and the coast-line of Asia Minor, which together gave the view overwhelming force. The bravery, military skill, and political freedom and innovations of the citizens of the Greek *poleis* made them greatly superior, they felt, both to the strong and tough, but politically disorganised, peoples to the northeast of Greece (such as Thracians and Scythians), and equally to the many soft and weak Asiatic peoples mostly ruled by the Persian empire. All these peoples who enjoyed no political freedom or control over their lives at home were thought fit to be 'enslaved' in Greece, and even to benefit from their contacts with the superior Greek culture. This belief, applied to the subjects of the Persian Empire, may have been strengthened by the Greeks' awareness that Persian Kings routinely referred to all their subjects, including their high officials such as satraps, as their 'slaves'; for example the Greek version, preserved on stone, of a letter from King Darius to a satrap in Ionia uses the word *doulos* of the satrap (see Fornara, *Archaic Times* no. 12). This may also, along with the sharpening of the idea of the free citizen, have helped to make *doulos* from the early fifth century on, the standard and commonest Greek term for a slave.

Ideas and stereotypes of this sort can be found throughout Greek drama and the speeches of the orators, usually crudely asserted but occasionally (especially in some plays of Euripides) more subtly open to question. The connected purposes of Herodotus' *Histories* are to present the history and cultures of the peoples to the East with whom the Greeks came into contact (mostly the Persians and the people whom the Persians conquered or tried to conquer), and to give an account of the Great Persian Wars. It is built on very complex patterns of contrasts between Greek political systems and culture and those of the variously different non-Greek peoples he considers. Overall, the work suggests that the Greeks were able to defeat the much larger forces of the Persians because of their much greater commitment to fight for their *polis*-based conceptions of political freedom and because of their preparedness, in a crisis, to unite against the common threat.

Such ideas also play a significant part in an important work of fifth-century Greek 'scientific' theory, the *Airs, Waters, Places*, one of the collection of medical texts associated with the great founder of scientific medicine, Hippocrates, and written some time during the later fifth century BC. The unknown author offers two different types of explanation for the characteristics of the various peoples he considers. The first is the regularity or irregularity of climatic conditions; the second is the contribution made by the political and social institutions. Hence the Asiatic peoples are said to be less courageous, less warlike and weaker than Europeans, first because of climatic conditions, namely that the seasons are uniform and equable and without sudden changes of temperature which might stir up wild passions and harden resolve. But another, political, reason for these characteristics is then given, namely their *nomoi*, that is their customs, laws and political institutions. Since they are mostly ruled by kings they have much less incentive to be warlike, because the military service demanded of them 'necessarily involves suffering and death on behalf of their masters, far from their children, wives and other friends' (ch. 16). Hence the author holds that men who are naturally brave and courageous can be ruined by such *nomoi* (for example, perhaps, Greeks living under Persian rule), whereas those peoples in Asia (Greek and non-Greek) who live independently of despotism are the bravest in all Asia. Similarly, the Scythians' peculiarities are explained both by the (highly exaggerated) coldness and wetness of their climate, and by their nomadic and excessively equestrian habits. And other Europeans (he has Greeks above all in mind) are varied in physique because of the different climates: in character, they are often fierce, anti-social and spirited because of the changeableness of the climate, but it is also their political independence which explains why they are so brave and so prepared to risk death.

Fig. 11 On Athenian vases, ornamental tattoos on necks, arms and legs (as opposed to tattooed or branded marks imposed as punishment on runaway slaves) are often found, and indicate 'barbarian' women, especially those from Thrace. So these girls fetching water from a fountain are identified as Thracian slaves. An Attic water-vessel (*hydria*) by the Aegisthus Painter, c. 470 BC.

Overall, while the work shows an interest in making precise observations and seeking 'scientific' explanations, it can be seen grossly to exaggerate both the climatic variations and the effects of political systems in order to reach predictable conclusions about the differences between Asiatics, Greeks and Scythians. These conclusions, conveniently, served two purposes. First, they explained, as had Herodotus, the military superiority of Greek soldiers so evident – to Greek eyes – in the wars of the fifth century; and second, they justified the use of such inferior 'barbarians' as slaves in the Greek world. But of course the more these justifications were seen as fundamental, the more problematic became the continued enslavement in the Greek world of other Greeks.

Hints of a critique of slavery?

Similar climatic and political explanations of the inferiority of barbarians are found in the fourth century philosophies of Plato and Aristotle. But before considering their treatment of the issues, the very limited evidence for some intellectual challenges to the justification of slavery as 'natural' should be considered. The debate was largely conducted in terms of a number of basic 'polarities', contrasts between opposed terms, of which the most important were slave/free, Greek/non-Greek, and the major analytical tool of the Sophists, the distinction between *physis* (nature) and *nomos* (custom, law, habit or convention).

Until lately, it was held that Antiphon, one of the late fifth-century sophists, expressed radical views that attacked the validity or 'naturalness' of the distinctions between high and low birth and between Greek and barbarian, and hence was probably also questioning (in the name of the 'unity of mankind') the justification of the enslavement of non-Greeks. The evidence comes in fragments from his sophistic dialogue 'On Truth', found on a papyrus in Egypt. But a small extra fragment discovered recently has changed our view of his argument. Antiphon now seems to have been arguing that all men who approve of the laws (*nomoi*) of those around them, and disapprove of those further away, 'have been made barbarians with regard to each other'; but in fact men are all alike in their basic physiological natures and needs. It seems, then, that this relativist argument suggested that the Greeks were not alone – or necessarily right – in despising the laws and habits of other peoples, and treating them as 'barbarians'; and it was probably part of Antiphon's more general, rather amoral, position, which was to allow all men the right to pursue their own 'necessary' desires, which is the main point that is made elsewhere in this fragment. So there seems no reason now to think that Antiphon either attacked the distinction between high and low birth, or that he explicitly developed his point about the shared physical chararacteristics of all humans into a criticism of slavery.

The only certain fifth-century evidence for criticism of the justice of slavery is to be found in a number of statements made by various characters in the surviving plays of Euripides, or in similar fragments from his plays which are now lost. Of course, since they are statements made by characters in plays one cannot easily assume that these statements, or indeed the many opposing statements in his plays which assert the justice of the enslavement of foreigners by Greeks, represent the views of Euripides himself. But the plays do provide evidence that theoretical and provocative statements criticising some fundamental Greek attitudes and ideologies were made on the Athenian stage in the late fifth century, and it is reasonable to suspect that, as in other cases of radical ideas in Euripides, these theatrical debates were echoing ideas expressed by some of the more radical of the sophists. A few such opinions can be quoted here.

Two central points are made more than once. First, after scenes in which individual slaves show qualities of loyalty, intelligence or bravery equal, or superior, to those shown by free people, characters in the plays often conclude that the institution of slavery often operates unjustly, enslaving and degrading those who do not deserve it. For example, in the *Ion* a loyal slave, prepared to risk his life for his mistress, claims that

> One thing alone brings shame to the slaves,
> the name; apart from all of that, a slave is no worse
> than free men in anything, if he is good.
>
> (Euripides, *Ion* 855-7)

One should perhaps also note that in this passage (and in a similar one in *Helen* 726-33) the noble slave shows qualities of loyalty and devotion to the interests of his master which involve acceptance of his status as a slave. The same is probably true of another such statement, for which we have no context:

> For many slaves the name is shameful, but their minds have
> more freedom than the minds of those who are not slaves.
>
> (fr. 833)

Yet more radically, in his *Alexandros* (a play about the early life of Paris), it seems that Paris, who has been brought up as a slave, succeeds in his claim to be permitted to compete with the free men in heroic games at Troy. Interpretation of the fragments is not easy, but it looks as if the following views are expressed: all men originally had the same appearance; noble birth, free birth and race do not guarantee good moral qualities; and while some slaves are enslaved only in name, for others it is an appropriate fate.

Second, in plays focusing on the consequences of war for the defeated victims, great pity is aroused at the enslavement of the women and children, for example, of the house of Troy in *Andromache*, *Trojan Women* and *Hecuba*. These may have had the effect of causing Greeks some anxiety about the justice of enslaving those defeated in war. Further, since there is considerable emphasis, above all in the *Trojan Women*, on the injustice and callous cruelty of the victorious Greeks, and considerable sympathy for the terrible sufferings and humiliations of the Trojan women who are represented as 'barbarians' by the Greeks, serious questioning of the Greek-barbarian contrast and the orthodox view of the moral superiority of the Greeks is also a significant part of the effects of these plays.

We cannot now identify the sophistic sources of the ideas expressed in these plays. Aristotle started his discussion of the issues of slavery with an admission that there were those who argued that the whole institution was unnatural because the distinction between slave and free was a matter of *nomos* (agreed convention), not of *physis* (nature), and was also unjust because it was based on force (*Politics* 1253b15-23). But he gives no hint whether such ideas were expressed in the late fifth century or closer to his own time in the second half of the fourth century. One such statement of which Aristotle was aware was made by Alcidamas, a teacher of rhetoric and a rival to Isocrates as a pupil of the sophist Gorgias. Aristotle refers to a statement in Alcidamas' pamphlet written in defence of the Messenian ex-helots who had set up their new state in 370 BC, which proclaimed a universal precept about justice (Aristotle,*Rhetoric* 1373b19); and the relevant sentence is quoted by the ancient commentators (*Scholia*) on the passage: 'God left all men free; nature made no man a slave'. This far-reaching assertion was almost certainly used to condemn the long-standing injustice of the helot-system in Sparta. Moreover, it seems likely that sophistic use of the nature/convention distinction in relation to slaves and free men sharpened many Greeks' distaste for the enslavement of their fellow Greeks, and hence increased interest in the origins of the helot-system and sympathy for the Messenians and other Greeks enslaved in wars or by piracy. But we do not know which thinkers applied, as Aristotle says some did, these ideas to chattel slavery of non-Greeks, nor how far they may have pressed their conclusions. Did they admit that it was 'against nature', and 'unjust', but leave it there? Did they perhaps claim that though this was so, it was necessary and had to be accepted (as many philosophers and lawyers later, for example under the Roman Empire, were to argue)? Or did they go further and suggest that it should, however gradually, be abolished? We have to state firmly that on existing evidence we cannot be sure that anyone in classical Greece took that more radical step and proposed the abolition of chattel slavery. What we can be certain is that there was nothing remotely resembling an 'abolitionist movement'.

Slavery in Plato's thought

Plato did not offer an extended account and defence of slavery; but, as we saw in chapter 5, he offered some guidance on the treatment of slaves. He also made passing comments on the naturalness and propriety of slavery throughout his work. Furthermore, a number of his major ideas of the proper rule and hierarchy in society, and in the soul of the individual, are developed precisely in terms of the idea of the justified rule of masters over slaves.

First, it is perfectly clear that in both Plato's 'ideal states', the startlingly radical, if not fully detailed, account of the *Republic* (written perhaps during the 370s BC) and the more realistic and much more detailed *Laws* (his last work, worked on perhaps up to his death in 347 BC), slaves are assumed to be essential to the management of the good state. Indeed, in the *Laws*, as was suggested in chapter 5, Plato's proposed laws affecting slaves, and his advice on their treatment, are somewhat stricter than those current in the Athens of his time.

Second, it seems from a number of passages that Plato would justify slavery on the basis of the slave's fundamental mental inferiority. For example, he claims that there are, properly, two types of medical practice (*Laws* 720a-e). Doctors treat their free clients by constructing a history of the disease through detailed communication with the patients and their friends, and give careful instruction to them in the disease and the treatment to be followed; but they treat slaves swiftly, giving them no account of the disease but prescribing treatment peremptorily, 'like a tyrant'. He also suggests that by and large free doctors treated free patients, and slave assistant-doctors treated slave patients. However, it is interesting that the detailed records of treatments contained in the Hippocratic works do not bear out such a division of their work. Plato's reason for the practice he recommends is that slaves lack the mental capacity to understand principles or give reasons for their beliefs; they cannot be left to decide anything for themselves, but must always be told what to do, and compelled by force if necessary.

There are clear signs that Plato took such views because he accepted up to a point the basic ethnographic orthodoxy. For example, in the *Republic* (435d-6a) he deploys the accepted stereotypes of the Thracians, Scythians and northern peoples as especially spirited, the Greeks as rational and intelligent and the Phoenicians and Egyptians as keen on money-making, while in another work (*Statesman* 262d) he criticises the over-simple lumping together of all non-Greeks as sharing precisely the same inferior characteristics. Plato's preparedness, which he never fully defended, to assume that at least some barbarian peoples were mentally inferior to the Greeks was strongly reinforced by his keen desire to promote harmony between the Greek states and to encourage them to fight wars against 'barbarians' rather than against each other, to treat only the 'barbarians' as natural enemies, and to restrict the enslaving of the defeated enemy (as also the serious destruction of land and buildings) to wars against foreigners, not those between Greeks (*Republic* 469b-471c). The slaves in Plato's state would be predominately non-Greek, and considered 'naturally' inferior. At times, however, he writes as if slavery would be an appropriate punishment for any in a community who deserved it because they were hopelessly sunk in 'ignorance and feebleness' (*Statesman* 309a).

Thirdly, Plato's view that power should be held by the intellectual elite (the 'philosopher Kings' in the *Republic*), who alone have true knowledge and understanding of the nature of the world and of justice, is often expressed in ways that suggest that only the rulers have 'true' freedom to determine their own lives and the direction of the state; all the rest, he suggests, whether notionally free workers, soldiers, or actual slaves, are best placed in a relationship of subjection or slavery (*douleia*) to the rulers. That is to say, that while the distinction between slave and free in Plato's ideal communities remains fixed and firm, most of their free populations should obey their intellectual betters in a manner comparable to the way good slaves obey their masters. In a similar fashion, Plato divided the 'soul' of the individual into three parts. The best part, which should rule, is the capacity to reason and to understand true principles; the other two inferior parts, which should be controlled and obey the best part, are, first, the 'spirited', the seat of courage and the sense of personal honour, and, second, the seat of the desires. The soul should obey the same hierarchical rules as should the state, and hence the two worse parts should obey, like slaves, the rational part. It is those who find this difficult because they lack the developed powers of reason who must be compelled to obey the laws of society developed by those in whom reason does reign supreme. This seems to be the case even for Greeks, in whom the reasoning power is especially well developed. In these senses, then, the principle of justified slavery can be seen to hold a central place in some of the most important areas of Plato's thought.

Aristotle's defence of the theory of natural slavery

It was Aristotle, Plato's greatest pupil, who confronted directly the issue of the moral justification of slavery. His main account comes in the first book of his *Politics* (1253b-1255b, also available in *GARS* 2), written during the period 335-323 BC. He views slavery as a natural and necessary element in the city-state, which he saw as the social system in which men could achieve the best form of civilization and individually attain the good life. As we saw, he was aware that a few thinkers had challenged the naturalness of slavery. Nonetheless he defended the institution, and saw its growth as part of the necessary progress from loose collections of households or villages to the cohesive city-state. His defence, complex and thoughtful though it is, is flawed by fundamental contradictions and illogicalities, as well as by the standard Greek-centred contempt for foreigners and insensitivity to slaves. This is in fact only to be expected in an attempt rationally to defend what seems to us to be patently indefensible. It is a testimony to the force of the ideological need to defend a basic social institution that such a profound and often fair-minded thinker was content with such weak arguments.

Unlike Plato, Aristotle did not see the rule of master over slave as the model for other types of rule or hierarchy. He carefully distinguished the rule of masters over slaves from other types of rule such as husbands over wives, parents over children, and various types of political authority. Rule over slaves is 'despotic rule', operating essentially in the interest of the masters. His project in defending such 'rule' involved at least four distinct elements: first, to define the characteristics and deficiencies that made some people suited only to be 'natural slaves'; second, to establish that sufficient numbers of identifiable people existed who fitted the role; third, to establish that these were the people who, mostly, were in fact employed as slaves in Greece; and fourth, to establish what form of slave-management would be effective and beneficial to both members of the master–slave relationship. In commenting briefly on how well Aristotle carried out this project, I shall bring out how his conception of the nature of the slave changes in the course of the arguments. The contradictions we have already noted in the images which other Greeks had of slaves, seeing them as tools, as animals, as perpetual children, or as almost like free humans, can be shown to cause decisive difficulties in Aristotle's account too.

Aristotle starts his account by saying that slaves are human beings who belong completely to their masters. He sees them as living pieces of property, who operate in ways comparable to the inanimate tools the master also possesses, but suggests that since slaves help us in many of our activities, they should not be defined as tools for production, but rather as tools for action. Slaves, like other humans – but also like animals – have a body and a mind (or soul). Hence slaves naturally suited for slavery should possess both a body suitable for their tasks – i.e. a body suited for indoor, bending-down activities (but less suited for military, farming or community activities), and also have the mental capacity to 'share in reason sufficiently to understand it, but not to possess it themselves'. Hence, like Plato, Aristotle holds that natural slaves were seriously deficient in the mental powers to make their own decisions and develop their own arguments, and so benefited by being permanently controlled and commanded by their masters. But what is involved in this idea of 'lacking reason' is not always clear, as there are significant variations in his images of the slave. Sometimes natural slaves seem to him to be little better than tame animals, or to relate to their masters as the body relates to the mind, as beings able only to respond to simple commands and happiest when simply obeying their masters. In other parts of his argument he thinks of them as closer to children (which was also a common Greek view), capable both of logically understanding the reasons for doing things, and of being trained to feel the correct emotions. The failure to sort out these differing conceptions has fatal results for his argument.

As for the second element in the project, Aristotle's theory requires that 'nature' should provide an abundant supply of easily identifiable people whose bodies were fit for slavish work, and whose minds lacked full reasoning powers. He recognises, however, that nature very often fails to achieve both of these aims; for example, he notes that many with the minds of free men have less than ideal bodies. In deciding who should be slaves, he puts a greater weight on the mental criterion; but he does note the difficulty that this mental deficiency is less easily observable than are physical weaknesses.

Where, then, does he think mentally inferior, natural slaves are to be found? He is less explicit than he might be on this, but it is in fact clear that he agrees with the standard classical Greek view that it is the 'barbarian' peoples who provide them. One of the major problems he admits – which gives strength to the view that slavery is only 'conventional', not 'natural' – is that slaves are often created as a result of wars, and that this often leads to the 'wrong' people being enslaved. Even if one takes the view (about which he has in any case strong doubts) that victory in war suggests the excellence of the victors (which might or might not include their justice), many of those thus enslaved would not be so clearly inferior as to be natural slaves. Such people, Aristotle agrees, can be seen as only slaves by convention (*nomos*), not by nature (*physis*). The true natural slaves are evidently various peoples of the non-Greek world, although which peoples he had in mind are not made clear in this passage. Elsewhere in the *Politics*, however, he presents ethnographic views very like those given by the Hippocratic author and by Plato quoted above (see pp. 87ff. and 92ff.). The non-Greek Europeans and those living in cold areas are spirited, but lack intelligence, so that they live as free peoples but without political organisation; Asiatics have intelligence and craft skills, but lack spirit and live under a form of rule that is called 'slavery'; the Greeks – in the middle – have the virtues both of spirit and intelligence, and hence 'the Greek race lives in freedom, has the best political organisation, and would be able to rule all others, if it could attain a single political unity' (1327b18-33). And, in another place, the barbarians generally are said to be 'more slave-like' than the Greeks, and among barbarians the Asiatics more so than the Europeans, because they endure despotic rule without discontent (1285a19-24). The 'natural slaves' seem thus to be identified, and it is their political weakness or anarchy at home which justifies their enslavement. However there is a clear contradiction here: the supposed general deficiency in the capacity to reason mentioned in Book 1 does not cohere with the failure in spirit, though not in intelligence, that makes the Asiatics apparently those foreigners most suited to slavery.

On the third element, it is evident that Aristotle holds that for the most part in Greece those enslaved are the proper ones. This amounts to the view that it is in general wrong for Greeks to be enslaved, but proper for non-Greeks. In this, as we saw, he is at one with Plato and with a growing feeling in Greece during the fourth century. Whether he thought that there were some Greeks so deficient in reasoning capacities (and/or in spirit) that they too deserved to be slaves, seems not to emerge clearly from the text. Overall, then, Aristotle did accept, pretty uncritically, the blanket condemnation of non-Greeks and the extremely crude stereotyping of different non-Greek races common in his world. This attitude can equally be seen in his famous advice to his pupil, Alexander the Great, that he should treat the barbarians he was engaged in conquering as slaves and animals.

In Aristotle's treatment of the management of slaves – the fourth element in the project – the inconsistences and contradictions in his view emerge even more clearly. Only if 'natural slaves' have throughout their lives extremely limited mental capacities can it conceivably be justified to treat them in a uniquely 'despotic' way. In such cases, one would, presumably, simply give them orders, and there could be no question of any 'friendship' existing. In places Aristotle does take this view (for example, in *Nicomachean Ethics* 1161a32-3): because there is no justice or community in the relationship, there can be no friendship. In the passage in Book 1 of the *Politics*, however, he allows that there can be some sort of friendship if the slave is a 'natural slave', and, presumably, believes that the relationship benefits him or her as well as the master. But in many places Aristotle implicitly recognises that there were many aspects of master–slave relationships, and advantageous ones, which were based on a different conception of slave capacities. He suggests that slaves need to have some small amount of appropriate 'virtue' developed by their masters, and hence be given reasons for their instructions, and not merely told what to do. He notes that some slaves act as foremen or overseers, with independence and some 'rule' of their own (1255b35-6); he asserts in the passage of the *Nicomachean Ethics* that one may develop friendship with a slave not inasmuch as he is a slave, but inasmuch as he is a man, which brings out the fundamental contradiction very clearly; and as we saw above, he advocates the use of manumission as a incentive for all slaves (*Politics* 1330a32-3), which is of course the single most glaring contradiction – and one firmly based in the institution – in the whole theory of the natural slave. If the slave was benefited by being a slave, freeing him would be unjust; if he had the potential to be free, he should be treated from the start more like a child needing training and development than like an animal. Thus we see that in these latter arguments Aristotle is operating with quite different models, in which the slave is potentially at least fully human, and his potential can be developed to the point where he can enjoy a limited degree of liberty as a freedman. But these models, while it may reflect aspects of the treatment offered to some privileged slaves, cannot justify the despotic rule which remained the basis of the whole slave system.

The many contradictions the account reveals are, in fact, those inherent in the practical workings of the slave system in Greece (and in many other slave-owning states). Aristotle's attempt to defend the indefensible usefully brings them out into the open. The evidence of his will, preserved, as are many others, in Diogenes Laertius' *Lives of the Philosophers*, is interesting, if it is genuine; though some scholars think that all the philosophers' wills thus preserved are later compilations. As it stands, it suggests that as an individual master he treated some at least of his slaves as more than 'natural slaves', and did (as he advised at *Politics* 1330a32-3) offer all his slaves the incentive of manumission. Some of his thirteen slaves are to be freed immediately, and set up securely, with slaves of their own; others are to be set free similarly on his daughter's marriage; and the rest are not to be sold, but to be still employed, and 'set free when they reach the right age if they deserve it' (5.11-16 = *GARS* 95).

Chapter 8
Associated Ideologies:
Work, Leisure and Sex

Consciousness of slaves, and the need to avoid seeming slave-like, permeated Athenian society. In this final chapter I take a brief look at the effects of this obsession on other attitudes and practices of Athenian male citizens, in particular on their attitudes to the conditions of labour and the pursuit of pleasures.

The slave-free distinction and Athenian attitudes to work

It was argued in chapter 4 that whether or not most ordinary Athenian peasant-farmers owned slaves at some time in their lives, slave-owning was universally regarded as a highly desirable thing. All Athenian citizens sought to have at least one or a few slaves. But even if they failed to own any, one essential condition of earning a living that preserved a citizen's status and sense of identity was to be in charge of own's own farm or business, not to be working 'for the benefit of another'.

Attitudes in Athens to different types and conditions of work were complex and, as in most societies, reflected the social prejudices and hostilities of different social classes of the population. But what matters here is to observe that the varied attitudes are all deeply affected by the very evident presence of slaves in all sectors of the economy, and also that these attitudes had a definite effect on the patterns of work under-taken and on the possibilities of advance for certain of the slaves themselves.

Greek cities developed essentially as communities of peasant-farmers, and hence the ideal that the typical citizen-soldier was an independent, nearly self-sufficient, farmer was deeply rooted in their social values. As we saw earlier, however, in Athens the major economic development of craft and manufacturing work, silver-mining and trad-ing, retailing and other activities associated with the city and the port of Piraeus, coincided with the developments of democracy, the sharpening of the division between citizens and foreigners by the creation of the status of metics, and the development of chattel slavery. All these developments operated together in mutually reinforcing ways to help create both the complex of attitudes evident in classical Athens and the standard forms of its economic life.

Firstly, farming remained the most common, and the most reputable, basis for wealth and means of making a living. Only citizens could own land or houses (hence metics, including freedmen, could only farm as tenant farmers, and had to rent their homes), and most citizens did own some land. In the fifth century there was considerable social prejudice against those (like the politician Cleon) whose wealth was based on the ownership of manufacturing slaves – a prejudice which seems to have abated somewhat by the fourth century. But members of the leisured classes continued to sneer more vigorously at those citizens engaged in crafts and manufacture than at poorer farmers. One form this prejudice took was a comparison between types of work. Farming work, outside in the open air, was held to be more gentlemanly, more 'masculine' and a better preparation for military action, than working inside a small workshop, indoors, in cramped, often smelly and in fact no doubt very dangerous conditions. Manufacturing would seem both more 'slavish' work, and in slightly different ways more 'womanly' work, than agriculture. Traders and shopkeepers encountered a different form of prejudice from the more prosperous groups, based on the view that living by buying and selling encouraged misrepresentation and cheating to make profits instead of creating wealth out of the land (the fact that producers also had to sell their goods was usually ignored in these arguments).

But a much more important and influential creator of prejudice and anxiety was the conditions under which people worked. Most ordinary Athenians expected and valued hard work (though they no doubt all aspired to a life of greater leisure); but they all objected to work which led them to being considered as slaves. In effect what this meant was that they felt it of the greatest importance to 'be their own boss', if possible owning slaves themselves, and not to work under the command and for the benefit of others.

These attitudes can be seen, slightly conflated, in a sentence from Aristotle's *Rhetoric* where he is seeking to encapsulate briefly standard Greek views on what is noble or honourable: 'Among the things that are honourable is not working in any vulgar craft; for it is the condition of a free man not to live for the benefit of another' (1367a32-3). The phraseology – 'vulgar (*banausos*) craft' – is that often used by the leisured class to condemn craft and manufacturing as menial or degrading; but the reason given uses the slave-free distinction, and would be accepted by all free Greeks, and applied to all forms of making a living. To work for another was what slaves did, and those who were forced to operate as hired labourers were likely to feel such conditions of work as slavish, and be attacked as slaves, or virtual slaves, by their enemies.

There are many consequences of the widespread acceptance of these attitudes. First, there was a certain amount of free hired or wage labour available in Athens, and there was a special spot assigned in the city (the *Kolonos Agoraios*) where men for hire congregated each day; but such labour remained very limited and undeveloped and attracted essentially only the very poor. Even they might well prefer to work in short term jobs rather than in permanent employment. This is well illustrated in one of Xenophon's Socratic conversations. Eutheros, an Athenian who once had properties in the Athenian Empire, is so poor after the end of the Peloponnesian War that he is earning a little money as best he can in manual work, presumably doing odd, short-term jobs for people. Socrates suggests that he might take a more permanent job as an overseer for a landowner, since that would provide more security, especially for his old age. Eutheros' response is that 'I would find it very hard being a slave, Socrates'. When Socrates suggests that those who manage the affairs of the city are thought to be the more 'free', not the more 'slavish', Eutheros pays no attention to this inaccurate parallel, and replies: 'In brief, Socrates, I have absolutely no desire to be subject to some one else's accounting'. Socrates answers that it is better to be subject to one considerate employer than a succession of potentially hard-to-please ones, as well as more secure (Xenophon, *Memorabilia* 2.8).

In some of the surviving law-court speeches we see what shame and disaster for the family could follow if members of it had to resort to hired labour or do other 'degrading' jobs, and how dangerous it could be to one's status as a citizen. For example, an attack on the heartless behaviour of a grasping citizen called Dicaiogenes emphasises this point:

> he stripped some of us of our property because he was stronger
> than we were, and others he stood by and watched as they went
> to be hired labourers through their lack of necessities.
>
> (Isaeus, 5.39)

Again, in 346/5 BC, at a major general revision of the citizenship-lists kept by all the demes throughout Attica, one Euxitheos was expelled from the list at a meeting of his deme Halimous. We have the speech he delivered (Demosthenes, 57) in order to reverse this decision before an

Athenian jury. His enemies attacked his supposed parents as being very poor and his father as having a foreign appearance, and used that to suggest that he, Euxitheos, was of foreign or slave birth, arguing either that his father was an ex-slave, or perhaps that his real father – a richer metic – had persuaded a poor couple to pass him off as their son, and hence a citizen (it is not quite clear from the defence what the attack was). Part of the material paraded also consisted of the 'facts' that his supposed mother had worked as a wet-nurse, and had sold ribbons in the market-place. Euxitheos' defence first accounts for his father's appearance by claiming that he had been captured during the latter stages of the Peloponnesian War and had spent some time as a slave on the island of Leucas before being ransomed back by his relatives. He also admits that when the family was in great financial difficulties his mother had indeed had to work as a wet-nurse for a rich family, and had had to sell in the market-place, but that this did not at all imply that she was foreign or slave. He points out that there was a specific provision in the law of slander protecting citizens and wives or daughters of citizens from being abused because they worked in the market-place (57.30-3). It is of course very significant that the Athenians felt it necessary to pass such a law to protect its poorer citizens, but it reveals that some Athenian men and women did work in the market, though mostly as independent operators.

Euxitheos seems to fear that the allegation of wet-nursing is more damaging. He admits that it was extremely unfortunate that his family had to engage in such activities:

> Maybe a wet-nurse is indeed a lowly thing; I do not run away from the truth. We have not done wrong just by being poor, but only if we were not citizens; the present trial is not about fortune or money, but about birth. Poverty compels free men to perform many slavish acts, for which, Athenians, they would more justly be pitied than further destroyed. I hear that in those times, because of the misfortunes of the city, many women of citizen families became wet-nurses, loom-workers and vineyard-workers, and many of those who were poor then are now rich.
>
> (Demosthenes, 57.45)

It can thus readily be understood that because citizens or free-born metics would seek at all costs to avoid taking on the sorts of jobs that incurred the designation 'slavish' and similar abuse, such jobs tended to be undertaken largely by slaves and freedmen. This set of attitudes is a major reason why, as we saw earlier, jobs such as overseers or bailiffs

Fig. 12 Athenian men enjoying, or about to enjoy, the evident pleasures of a *symposion*, on a fifth-century vase, painted, like Fig. 8, by the Foundry Painter. The naked flute-girl is presumably to be imagined as hired for the party, and is likely to be a slave.

on farms, or as agents, organisers and managers in manufacturing, trade and banking, created opportunites for some slaves to work independently. Such slaves could make some money, and perhaps could earn their freedom young enough to have a good chance of making a success in the business in which they had been trained.

This process meant that potential gaps in the economy, into which the citizens were reluctant to move because of the overwhelming desire not to work for another, were filled variously by slaves, freedmen and some metics; and, on the whole, there was not a strong sense of competition or envy between the different status-groups, even though a few metics and ex-slaves became conspicuously very rich. We do not hear cries from the free poor that 'their jobs' were being taken by slaves or ex-slaves; by and large they did not wish to take on those jobs.

Slavery and citizens' attitudes to pleasures, sex, women and boys

In a different and rather more metaphorical way many Athenians wished to avoid seeming 'slavish' through being too dependent on their own desires and passions, particularly those associated with the body. One powerful ideal of the citizen was to be brave, independent and

UWE. BRISTOL LIBRARY SERVICE

self-controlled, maintaining oneself in a fit condition to manage one's farm or business, and to fight for the city. Hence too much indulgence in the pleasures of food, drink, sex and the life of luxury was held to be deplorable because it weakened one's bodily strength and fitness. It was also condemned because it threatened to waste the resources of the family to the detriment of one's heirs, and meant spending money on oneself which was better spent (if one was rich enough) for the benefit of the city, for example in the form of the 'liturgies', the public services supporting Athens' fleet or her festivals. There was, of course a significant conflict of values here, since Athenians naturally wanted to become richer than their fellows, partly to be able to enjoy their wealth in expensive, and conspicuous, pleasures. One common way to condemn excessive indulgence in expensive pleasures was to describe it as enslaving oneself, or one's soul, to the domination of the baser desires and pleasures, or to the worse parts of one's own self. Such language is found not only in philosophical moralists like Plato and Aristotle but also in the more ordinary language of the law-court speeches. It was a particularly powerful argument in a society where 'slavery' was so evidently a condition to be avoided at all costs. For example, as part of a sustained attack on a political opponent for his sexual activities in his youth (on which see also below) Aeschines says this about Timarchos:

> His father had left him a very substantial property which he had himself devoured, as I shall show as my speech proceeds. He did these things because he was a slave to the most shameful pleasures, elaboration and extravagance of dinners, flute-girls and call-girls (*hetairai*), dicing and the other activities, none of which ought to get the better of any man who is well-born and free.

> (Aeschines, 1.42)

Thus a man who indulged himself too 'freely', as we might say, in pleasures and luxury was often said to be behaving in a 'slavish' way; by being enslaved to his appetites he was no longer really free. This mode of argument was later (in Hellenistic and Roman times, and also much later) to become a comforting way for slaveowners to respond to questions of the injustice of slavery. The important issue, it would be claimed, for example, by both Stoics or Christians, was not whether one was legally a slave to another man, but whether one's soul was 'free' to be good and follow God's law, or was 'enslaved' to one's desires or the forces of Evil.

But Athenian citizens liked to think their women and children were more likely to be so 'enslaved' to desires than they were themselves. We can look at the Athenian city as a large participatory democracy in which something like 30,000 citizens shared much of the power; but it is also proper to view it as a rather exclusive 'club' to which only free males born of two Athenian parents were admitted. Hence the citizen lived surrounded by different categories of people to whom he felt superior and over whom he exercised different types of authority: women, children, metics and slaves. Intellectuals like Plato and Aristotle argued about the degree of similarity or difference between the different types of rule or authority over these different categories. The ordinary citizen operated with conventionally accepted rules for the members of his household, and sought to ensure that the proper boundaries of behaviour between these separate categories were maintained. If we explore some of these rules and practices we can see a number of ways in which Athenian males used these 'polarities' of free/slave, man/woman or adult/child, to formulate their self-identities by contrast with others, thereby fostering their sense of their own superiority by their beliefs that children and women were 'naturally' closer to slaves than they were, and hence needed almost as careful a scrutiny.

It would certainly be an exaggeration to state that Athenians regarded their wives as little better than slaves, and treated them accordingly. Free women were as carefully distinguished from slave women in their privileges and their duties as were free men. But most Athenian men did try, as far as their financial circumstances allowed, to keep their daughters and wives away from associating with adult males who were not their relatives. Above all they imposed on them, before and after marriage, strict codes of chastity and marital fidelity in order to preserve the reputation of the family, and to prevent there being any hint of doubt about the parentage of the children. Among the reasons they offered for such protectiveness, for the fact that a respectable woman had to have a male relative in authority over her as her legal guardian (*kyrios*) throughout her life, and for women's exclusion from all political life, were certain beliefs about women's 'nature'. Women were thought to derive more pleasure from sex than men, and to be more lacking in moral self-control; hence, as a fragment of a comic poet puts it, it was a common belief that 'To be enslaved to pleasure is the behaviour of a licentious woman, not of a man' (Anaxandrides, fr. 60 Kock). Equally, women were widely supposed to be more likely than men to be 'enslaved' to the pleasures of food and especially drink, to be excessively emotional, to be weak, cowardly and fearful, and to be unable to develop rational arguments – in short to be generally inferior. In all these respects slaves were regarded as being even more inferior to free men. It follows that women's natures were conceived as being closer to slaves than were those of their menfolk. In consequence, they needed to be carefully watched by those in authority over them; though most Athenian men would probably agree with Aristotle that the nature and methods of their rule over women was different from, and less severe than, those they used with their slaves.

The self-serving absurdity of these attitudes does not need to be emphasised. One may observe, however, that Athenian society maintained a firm separation of the female sex into (a) the respectable women, who should marry and produce legitimate children, and (b) the various types of less respectable women, most of whom were slaves, ex-slaves or metics (prostitutes, concubines, flute-girls, *hetairai* etc.), with whom men could have sexual relations of varying degrees of regularity and passion. This compartmentalising of women, and the existence of slaves as sex-objects, coupled with their beliefs about women's self-indulgent natures, enabled men to satisfy their own desires for sexual satisfaction and even for emotional 'affairs' outside marriage, while imposing very strict rules on the women of their families. The main limits to such male exploitation of this 'double standard' were set not so much by feelings of respect towards their wives as by the beliefs mentioned above that one should not waste the family's resources, damage one's body or deprive the community of its 'liturgies' by excessive extravagance.

Many free children in Athens were partly brought up by their slave nurses and *paidagogoi*; but they quickly had to learn that they were legally and morally their superiors, and that growing up involved learning not to behave like the slaves who (if male) were called 'boy' throughout their lives. One particular area of moral delicacy for a boy or youth growing up in Athens occurred if he were attractive enough to be pursued by an older Athenian male who wished to be his lover. Here especially he was expected to take care to avoid being condemned for behaving like a woman or a slave.

Classical Greeks did not share the assumption, common in modern European societies, that individuals have a settled disposition to be exclusively heterosexual or homosexual in their 'orientation'. City-states expected all citizens to marry and have children, but it was generally thought that many or perhaps most males might feel sexual desire for other males as well as for females. Further – originally for historical reasons which are not at all clear – a particular type of homosexual relationship in which older males, usually in their twenties and still unmarried, loved somewhat younger youths or boys was regarded in Athens with tolerance or even with approval. Such relationships were, it seems, especially common among the wealthier classes. These 'pederastic' relationships were typically regarded as 'asymmetrical', not reciprocal, in that the older 'lover' (*erastes*) sought to persuade the younger 'beloved' (*eromenos*) or 'boy' or 'boyfriend' (*pais, paidika*) to grant him sexual favours in exchange for companionship and some helpful education or introduction to adult male society (especially in the *gymnasia* and at the drinking parties). The older partner took the initiative and was more active, sexually and socially, the younger more receptive and passive. But there were serious risks in such relationships, especially for the 'beloved', and these could be expressed in terms of his behaving in a 'slavish', or 'womanly' fashion.

The social dangers for the lovers were essentially the same as for those engaged in other forms of the pursuit of pleasure, those of being seen to be enslaved to their desires, or to the whims of the loved one, and of wasting their resources and failing to behave correctly to their families and to the city. The beloved ran graver dangers. Legally, if a youthful son of a citizen engaged in activities that could be labelled as self-prostitution, that is as selling himself for sexual use by others, he was not held to have committed a crime as such (there were other laws protecting minors and youths against rape and enforced prostitution); but such a youth was considered to have shown himself permanently unfit to be a fully active citizen. A penalty would only follow if he later sought to hold any public office, prosecute in a political case, or speak in the assembly or the council, and then only if an enemy of his decided to indict him. How often this happened is not clear (probably very seldom), but one such case was the successful prosecution of Timarchos by Aeschines in 346/5 BC. Aeschines' speech emphasises the ease with which the youthful Timarchos agreed to act as the passive partner in a succession of such relationships, and his readiness to live off his lovers in order to finance his own extravagant desires. These faults are held to show that he was behaving in a slavish and womanly way in thus selling his body to serve the lusts of other men, since slaves often had to submit to any sexual demands of their masters or serve as prostitutes, and women too depended on men for their livings, were weaker and less self-controlled than men, and took passive roles in sexual intercourse (see, for example, Aeschines, 1.42, 75-6, 185).

For the same reasons, 'beloveds' had to be careful of social disapproval, as well as of a possible future prosecution. They should not be thought to be too easily persuaded to yield to their lovers or to move easily from one to another, in case they be held to be behaving too much like slaves or prostitutes; nor, probably, should they be thought to submit to anal penetration or to appear to enjoy the sex acts themselves. This seems to be a reasonable conclusion from the fact that the majority (though not quite all) of the many Greek vases that show lover and beloved sexually involved show the older copulating between the thighs of the younger, while the younger shows no sign of erection or pleasure – though this does not necessarily reflect at all closely what may actually have occurred in such relationships.

Conclusions

Thus these sexual relationships and attitudes, like so many other practices and beliefs in classical Athens, were deeply affected by the presence of slaves in so many citizen families, and by the consciousness of Athenians that at all costs they must avoid becoming slaves, being thought to be treated like slaves, or to behave like slaves. The extent to which Athenian civilization and its achievements did in fact depend on the use of slave labour is likely to remain a controversial question. But two important conclusions about Athenian society and its relation to slavery should not be matters of dispute. First, slavery was felt by Athenians to be so essential to the functioning of their society that the only – even imagined – alternatives to it seem to be fantastic suppositions of a Golden Age where all the work did itself (for example, in some passages from comedies, quoted by Athenaeus 267e-270a), or of work done by robot-like tools that obeyed orders (Aristotle, *Politics* 1253b33-54a1). No serious attempt was apparently ever made to propose the abolition of so obviously worrying an institution, and even the best thinkers of the time accepted very poor arguments to justify it. Second, the distinction between slave and free was one of the most fundamental and determining antitheses in the structures of thought and moral values of the Athenians (and probably of other Greeks). This polarity played a significant part in the Athenians' formation of their identities and ideals as free and independent men, and, as Greeks, more fully free and advanced than all foreigners. It also profoundly affected their attitudes and moral judgements over a whole range of economic, social and sexual matters. In these senses, then, slavery was undoubtedly a fundamental feature of Athenian society.

Suggestions for Further Study

1. What are the essential differences between chattel slaves and serfs? Which group do you think tended to receive more degrading treatment, and which could have greater hopes of an improvement in their conditions?

2. What sorts of information about slaves does archaeological evidence provide? What are the limitations of such evidence?

3. What criteria can we use to tell slaves from non-slaves in representations in sculpture and vase-painting?

4. How far can we tell the precise status of the agricultural workers and domestic servants in the Homeric poems? Are they fully chattel slaves, or more like serfs? Are they treated more favourably than slaves in classical Athens? If so, is that to be explained by the needs of the epic stories or does it reflect conditions during the Dark Ages?

5. 'The advance, hand-in-hand, of freedom *and* slavery' (Finley). How far can we understand and explain the abolition of debt-bondage and slavery for debts for citizens in Athens? How much can we learn from the contemporary evidence of Solon's own poems? How exactly was the liberation of citizens from forms of dependence connected with the increase in their participation in the government of their city? To what extent, if at all, were both these processes connected with the availability of foreign chattel slaves?

6. How much of the political institutions and policies of the Spartan state can be explained by their fears of a helot revolt? What attempts did the Spartans make to win the loyalty of some or all of the helots? Can we explain why the Messenian helots revolted more often than the Laconian helots, and why the latter did not seek their freedom in the aftermath of the Theban invasion of 370 BC?

7. Why is it so difficult to discover the extent to which slavery was used in different kinds of agriculture in the Athenian economy? Why did it

matter so much to Athenian citizens to be owners of at least one or two slaves? How expensive was it to acquire slaves, and how difficult was it to maintain them? How would the Athenian economy have been affected if foreign slaves had not been available?

8. Could the Athenian democracy have functioned without slaves?

9. Do you think the Athenian laws concerning the treatment of slaves showed any concern for slaves as human beings, or were they only concerned with the rights and honour of the citizens, and the value of the slaves as property? How much can we believe what is said in the treatises on household management of the uses and treatment of slaves? Do you agree that the regulations and the advice on handling slaves show the society's confused and contradictory conceptions of the nature of slaves?

10. How far is it possible to work out rates of manumission for Athens or for any other society in ancient Greece? Was manumission often a bad deal for the ex-slaves in Greece, and if so why did slaves want to be freed?

11. To what extent, in the absence of direct evidence for the feelings of slaves in Greece, is it possible for us to understand the 'consciousness' of the slaves? How much evidence do we have for relationships of loyalty and friendship, and how much for feelings of bitterness and hatred? How important was religion in the lives and emotions of the slaves? Did religion help slaves to conform with their masters' wishes or to combine together to resist them?

12. How far were the Greeks under pressure to justify slavery to themselves? Would you call their attitudes to non-Greeks, as 'barbarians' and fit for slavery, racist? To what extent did they seek to find 'evidence' to support these attitudes?

13. What other areas of economic life and social relations were affected by the existence of slavery in Athenian society? Why did the free poor in Greece not seem to feel common solidarity with the slaves? In what ways did Athenian men think their women were apt to resemble slaves in nature or behaviour?

14. Should we conclude that slavery was a basic element giving Greek civilization its fundamental shape?

Suggestions for Further Reading

Sources and collections of texts in translations:

In general, many of the texts discussed can be found in Penguin Classics and more in the Loeb Classical Library. The main source-book for ancient slavery, cited throughout in this book, is Thomas Wiedemann's *Greek and Roman Slavery* (Routledge, 1981), though it contains more material on the Roman side than on the Greek. Other useful sourcebooks for Greek social history are:

Austin, M., and Vidal-Naquet, P., *Economic & Social History of Ancient Greece* (Batsford, 1977).

Fisher, N.R.E., *Social Values in Classical Athens* (Dent, 1976).

Fornara, C., *Archaic Times to the End of the Peloponnesian War: Translated Documents of Greece and Rome* (Cambridge University Press, 1983).

General books

Wiedemann, T., *Slavery: Greece and Rome New Surveys in the Classics* 19 (Oxford, 1987; 2nd edn, 1993) [excellent brief survey of issues and recent work].

Garlan, Y., *Slavery in Ancient Greece* (Cornell, 1988) [best general account by excellent French historian in the 'post-Marxist' tradition].

Finley, M.I., *Ancient Slavery and Modern Ideology* (Penguin, 1980) [penetrating analysis of the history of the subject, and of all the central issues, by one of the most influential ancient historians working on slavery since World War II].

de Ste. Croix, G.E.M., *The Class Struggle in the Ancient Greek World from the Archaic Age to the Arab Conquests* (Duckworth, 1981) [massive, discursive and idiosyncratic application of Marxist analysis to the ancient world].

Finley, M.I. (ed.), *Slavery in Classical Antiquity* (Heffer, 1968) [collection of valuable articles: see especially those by Finley, 'Was Greek Civilization based on Slave Labour'; Vlastos, 'Slavery in Plato's Thought'; and Schlaifer, 'Greek Theories of Slavery from Homer to Aristotle'].

Vogt, J., *Ancient Slavery and the Ideal of Man* (Blackwell, 1974) [collection of essays by leading German scholar, founder of the Mainz Akademie research programme on slavery; especially strong on the evidence for slaves' reactions, whether of loyal service or of revolt].

Patterson, O., *Slavery and Social Death* (Harvard University Press, 1982) [major world-wide comparative analysis of the social effects of slave-systems].

Homer and the Archaic Age

Finley, M.I., *The World of Odysseus*^{2} (Penguin, 1977) [epoch-making analysis of 'Homeric society', dated to the ninth century BC; perhaps seems now to give too simplified and coherent a picture].

Snodgrass, A., *Archaic Greece* (Dent, 1980) and Murray, O., *Early Greece* (Fontana, 1980) [good general accounts of archaic Greek history].

For more detailed and controversial treatments of the Homeric poems as evidence for Dark Age society see:

Quiller, B., 'The Dynamics of the Homeric society' *Symbolae Osloenses* 56 (1981) 109-55.

Morris, I.M., 'The Use and Abuse of Homer' *Classical Antiquity* 5 (1986) 81-138.

Van Wees, H., *Status Warriors* (Gieben, 1992).

For more detailed and controversial treatments of early Athenian agriculture, society and Solon's reforms:

Finley M.I., *Economy and Society in Ancient Greece* (Chatto & Windus/Penguin, 1981/3) chs 7-9, and *Ancient Slavery and Modern Ideology* ch. 2.

Morris, I.M., *Burial and Ancient Society* (Cambridge University Press, 1987).

Gallant, T.W., 'Agricultural systems, land tenure and the reforms of Solon' *Annual of the British School at Athens* 7 (1982) 111-24.

Manville, P.B., *The Origins of Citizenship in Ancient Athens* (Princeton, 1990) chs 5 and 6.

On Solon's laws to do with *hybris* and *gymnasia*, see the articles by N.R.E. Fisher and O. Murray in *NOMOS: essays in Athenian law, politics and society* (Cambridge University Press, 1990) 123-38, 139-46.

Sparta and other Serf-systems

Discussions of the distinction between slaves and other types of dependence, and of the Spartan helots as a class, in the articles by G.E.M. de Ste. Croix and P. Cartledge in L. Archer (ed.), *Slavery and other Forms of Unfree Labour* (Routledge, 1988) 19-32, 33-41.

On Spartan society as a whole, and the helot-system within it:

Finley, M.I., *Economy and Society in Ancient Greece* ch. 2 [good brief analysis of Spartan society].

de Ste. Croix, G.E.M., *Origins of the Peloponnesian War* ch. 4 [major treatment of Sparta's political and social system].

Cartledge, P., *Sparta and Laconia* [good political and economic history of Sparta, with full emphasis (esp. ch. 10) on 'class-struggle' between Spartiates and helots].

Cartledge, P., *Agesilaos and the Crisis of Sparta* (Duckworth, 1987) esp. ch. 21 [concentrates analysis on the fourth-century crisis at Sparta].

See also the following essays, analysing in more detail aspects of the social and economic relations between Spartiates and helots:

Hodkinson, S., 'Social order and the conflict of values in classical Sparta' *Chiron* 13 (1983) 239-81.

Powell, C.A., *Athens and Sparta* (Routledge, 1988) chs 3 and 6.

Powell, C.A. (ed.), *Classical Sparta: Techniques behind her Success* (Routledge, 1989) [a set of articles demonstrating Sparta's devices for holding its society together: those by David, Fisher, Hodkinson and Powell are particularly relevant].

For boys' initiation rituals in Sparta and elsewhere in Greece, see P. Vidal-Naquet, 'The Black Hunter and the origin of the Athenian *ephebeia*', and 'Recipes for Greek adolescence', in *Myth, Religion and Society*, R.L. Gordon (ed.) (Cambridge, 1981) 147-62, 163-85, and also in *The Black Hunter* (Johns Hopkins, 1986) 106-28, 129-56.

Athenian Slavery

On the numbers, economic functions and the democracy:

The debate on agricultural slavery can be followed in:

Jones, A.H.M., *Athenian Democracy* (Blackwell, 1957) 3-20 [survey of evidence, arguing for low numbers and importance of slaves, and minimal use of slaves on the land].

At the other extreme:

Jameson, M.H., 'Agriculture and Slavery in Classical Athens', in *Classical Journal* 73 (1977-8) 122-46 [the fullest case for very extensive use of slaves in agriculture: see also the briefer statement in G.E.M. de Ste. Croix, *Class Struggle* 133ff., 506ff.].

A counter to this, explicitly seeking to acquit most Athenian peasant democrats from the charge of slave-ownership, is: E.M. Wood, *Peasant Citizen and Slave* (Verso, 1988) esp. ch. 2, and a similar position in: R. Osborne, *Demos: The Discovery of Classical Attika* (Cambridge University Press, 1985) esp. 142ff.

A sensible middle position is taken by:

Sinclair, R.M., *Democracy and Participation in Athens* (Cambridge University Press, 1988) esp. 196ff., and Hansen, M.H., *The Athenian Democracy in the Age of Demosthenes* (Blackwell, 1991) esp. 317ff.

The most recent and sophisticated assessments of ancient Greek peasant agriculture are R. Sallares, *The Ecology of the Ancient Greek World* (Duckworth, 1991) [argues for a mimimalist view of the use of slaves], and T.W. Gallant, *Risk and Survival in Ancient Greece* (Polity, 1991) [holds that many Athenian peasants might not be able to afford a slave all the time, but they would own them when they possibly could].

On slavery in mining, manufacture, building, etc., see:

Burford, A., *Craftsmen in Greek and Roman Society* (Thames & Hudson, 1972).

Isager, S. and Hansen, M.H., *Aspects of Athenian Society in the*

Fourth Century BC (Odense, 1975).

Hopper, R.J., *Trade and Industry in Classical Greece* (Thames & Hudson, 1979).

Osborne, R., *Demos: The Discovery of Classical Attika* chs 5 and 6.

On metics, see also D. Whitehead, *The Ideology of the Athenian Metic* (Cambridge Philological Society, 1977).

On the Athenian laws relating to slavery, and on public slaves, see briefly:

MacDowell, D.M., *Law in Classical Athens* (Thames & Hudson, 1978) 79ff.

Hansen, M.H., *The Athenian Democracy in the Age of Demosthenes* 120ff.

On cruelty and humanity in the treatment of slaves, see the contrasting studies of: J. Vogt, *Ancient Slavery and the Ideal of Man* and M.I. Finley, *Ancient Slavery and Modern Ideology* ch. 3.

On manumission, see the general points, with analysis of documents from Hellenistic Delphi, in K. Hopkins, *Conquerors and Slaves* (Cambridge University Press, 1978) ch. 3. [good treatment also of the growth and nature of Roman slavery in chs 1 and 2]; also O. Patterson, *Slavery and Social Death* ch. 8.

The Athenian manumission documents of the 330s are studied by D.M. Lewis in *Hesperia* 28 (1959) 208-38 and 37 (1967) 368-80.

On the slave-trade and piracy see:

Finley, M.I., 'The slave trade in antiquity' *Economy and Society in Ancient Greece* ch. 10.

Garlan, Y., 'War, Piracy and Slavery in the Greek World', in M.I. Finley (ed.), *Classical Slavery* (Cass, 1987) 7-20.

Resistance and Revolts

Cartledge, P., 'Rebels and Sambos in Classical Greece', in *CRUX: Essays for G.E.M. de Ste. Croix* (Imprint Academic, 1985) 16ff. [good general article, comparing the prevalence to resistance and revolt in

Athens, Sparta and other slave-systems, especially in the New World].

For revolts and slave-wars in the Roman world:

Vogt, J., *Ancient Slavery and the Ideal of Man* chs 3 and 4.
Bradley, K.R., *Slavery and Rebellion in the Roman World* (Indiana/Batsford, 1989).

Justifications and Ideologies

On the general development of theorising on slavery, see the article by Schlaifer in M.I. Finley (ed.), *Slavery in Classical Antiquity* 93-132.

On the idea of barbarians as natural inferiors and slaves:

Diller, A., *Race mixture among the Greeks before Alexander* (Illinois, 1937).
Hartog, F., *The Mirror of Herodotus: the Representation of the Other in the Writing of History* (University of California Press, 1988).
Hall, E., *Inventing the Barbarian: Greek Self-Definition through Tragedy* (Oxford, 1989).

On sophistic debates, and Euripides, see also:

Guthrie, W.K.C., *History of Greek Philosophy* Vol. III.1 (Cambridge, 1969, separately published as *The Sophists* [Cambridge, 1971]).

On fourth-century developments: P. Vidal-Naquet, 'Reflections on the Greek historiography of slavery', in *The Black Hunter*, 168-88.

On slavery in Plato, see the articles by G. Vlastos, 'Slavery in Plato's Thought', in M.I. Finley (ed.), *Slavery in Classical Antiquity* 133-49; also in *Platonic Studies* (Princeton University Press, 1973) 147-63, and 'Did slavery exist in Plato's *Republic*?' *Classical Philology* 63 (1968) 291-5, and in *Platonic Studies* 140-6.

On Aristotle's theories of slavery see articles by W.W. Fortenbaugh, 'Aristotle on Slaves and Women', in Barnes, Schofield, Sorabji (eds), *Articles on Aristotle* II (Duckworth, 1977) 135-9, and [better, in my view] N.D. Smith, 'Aristotle's Theory of Natural Slavery' *Phoenix* 37 (1983) 109-22, and G. Cambiano, 'Aristotle and the Anonymous Opponents of Slavery', in M.I. Finley (ed.), *Classical Slavery* 21-41.

On the relations between Athenian attitudes to slaves and to women and boys, see above all R. Just, *Women in Athenian Law and Life* (Routledge, 1989) esp. ch. 6 [good comparison of Athenian ideologies towards women, slaves and boys] and cf. also his article on 'Freedom, Slavery and the Female Psyche' in *CRUX* 169-188; K.J. Dover, *Greek Homosexuality* (Blackwell, 1978), and M. Golden, 'Slavery and Homosexuality in Athens' *Phoenix* 38 (1984) 308-24, and *Children and Childhood in Classical Athens* (Johns Hopkins, 1990)

Slavery in the Americas

Just a tiny selection of general works on this enormous topic:

Stampp, K., *The Peculiar Institution: Slavery in the Ante-Bellum South* (Random House, 1956).
Genovese, E., *Roll, Jordan, Roll* (Pantheon, 1974).
Blassingame, J.W., *The Slave Community* (Oxford University Press, 1979).
Fogel, R.W. and Engelman, S.L., *Time on the Cross* (Little, Brown & Co., 1974).
Goldin, C.D., *Urban Slavery in the American South* (University of Chicago Press, 1976).
Koger, L., *Black Slaveowners: Free Black Slave Masters in South Carolina, 1790-1860* (McFarland, 1985).

A narrative of an ex-slave: *Narrative of the Life of Frederick Douglass* (Penguin, 1982)

On slave resistance and revolts:

Patterson, O., 'Slavery and Slave Revolts: A Socio-Historical Analysis of the First Maroon War, Jamaica 1655-1740' *Social and Economic Studies* 19 (1970) 289-326.
Genovese, E., *From Rebellion to Revolution* (Louisiana State University Press, 1979).

On the 'problem of slavery' in Western intellectual traditions from the ancient world to the Americas:

Davis, D.B., *The Problem of Slavery in Western Culture* (Cornell/Penguin, 1966/70).

Davis, D.B., *Slavery and Human Progress* (Oxford, 1984).

Glossary

andrapodon, pl. -*a*: literally 'man-foot creature', referring to a slave essentially seen as an animal or a thing: see p. 7.

anthropos: 'human being', occasionally used to refer to a slave, often with the implication that s/he has no further social identity: see p. 7.

chattel slavery: the system of using captured or purchased slaves, effectively the property of individual owners: see especially pp. 3-6.

debt-bondsmen: those pledged to perform services to their creditors, with the hope of eventually paying off the debt: see pp. 4-5.

dmos, pl. *dmoes* (masc.), *dmoie*, pl. *dmoiai* (fem.): terms for slaves in Homer and archaic Greece: see pp. 10-14.

douleia 'slavery', *doulos* 'slave': common term (from the fifth century BC on the most common term) for slave, which emphasises in particular the status of slave as opposed to free, or to citizen: see especially pp. 6-7, 86f.

eleutheria 'freedom', *eleutheros* 'free': standard terms for the status of being free, not slave or otherwise dependent on others: see p. 6.

eranos: collective friendly contribution, e.g. for a common meal; often used for shared contributions to help a friend with an interest-free loan, e.g. to ransom from slavery, or to pay for the manumission of a slave: see pp. 36, 68.

freedman/woman: an ex-slave who has been manumitted. In Athens, they had metic-status: see especially pp. 67-71.

hektemoroi: 'sixth-parters', sharecropping peasants in pre-Solonian Athens: see pp. 15-17.

helots: the 'serfs' of Sparta, owned by the state, and mostly tied to labour on farms owned by individual Spartiates: see ch. 3.

hetaira: '(female)-companion': in Athens, they could be slaves, ex-slaves or foreign metics, women who served men's sexual needs outside marriage: the term sometimes includes all prostitutes, but often suggests more expensive 'courtesans' or those with a longer-lasting relationship with one man, or several: see pp. 55 and 103-6.

hybris: deliberately insulting and dishonouring behaviour: the Athenian law against *hybris* in theory protected slaves, women and children as well as male citizens: see pp. 17-18 and 63-4.

krypteia: 'secret operation', the Spartan institution for controlling and selectively killing helots: see pp. 28-30.

manumission: the formal setting free of slaves, often under restrictive conditions: see especially pp. 3, 67-71 and 97-8.

metics: status of foreigners in Athens who stayed longer than a set time (probably a month), and had to pay a poll-tax and have an Athenian as their legal representative. Manumitted slaves in Athens acquired metic-status: see pp. 20, 68.

oiketes: 'houseboy/girl', term occaissionally applied to all dependents in the household (*oikos*), but usually applied to slaves, often, but not always, slaves seen as part of the household: see p. 7.

paidagogos: domestic slave charged with attending and watching a free child: see pp. 55, 73-4, 106.

pais: 'boy', 'child', a term also regularly applied to slaves, of any age: see pp. 7, 71 and 106.

periokoi: 'livers-around', members of the self-governing communities inside the Spartan state, politically dependent on Sparta: see ch. 3.

polis, pl. *poleis*: 'city-state', the small-scale, independent state of archaic and classical Greece: see especially pp. 14-21.

serfs: tenant farmers tied to land they do not own: see p. 4.

Spartiates, -ai: Full Spartan citizens: see ch. 3.

symposia: formalised drinking parties, a characteristic feature of leisure activities in Greek culture: see pp. 17-18, 55, 104-7.

thes, pl. *thetes*: landless labourer of free status: see p. 12.